INDEPENDENT EVALUATION GROUP

D0516643

Analyzing the Effects of Policy Reforms on the Poor

An Evaluation of the Effectiveness of World Bank Support to Poverty and Social Impact Analyses

2010
The World Bank
Washington, D.C.

http://www.worldbank.org/ieg

Cover: A student at the public primary school Alvaro Contreras in Tegucigalpa, Honduras. Photo by Alfredo Srur, courtesy of the World Bank Photo Library.

ISBN-13: 978-0-8213-8293-6
e-ISBN-13: 978-0-8213-8294-6
DOI: 10.1596/978-0-8213-8293-6

Library of Congress Cataloging-in-Publication data have been applied for.

World Bank InfoShop
E-mail: pic@worldbank.org
Telephone: 202-458-5454
Facsimile: 202-522-1500

Independent Evaluation Group
Communications, Learning and Strategy
E-mail: ieg@worldbank.org
Telephone: 202-458-4497
Facsimile: 202-522-3125

 Printed on Recycled Paper

Contents

Boxes

Figure

Abbreviations

ADMARC	Agricultural Development and Marketing Corporation (Malawi)
CAS	Country Assistance Strategy
CPA	Chittagong Port Authority (Bangladesh)
DFID	Department for International Development (United Kingdom)
DPL	Development Policy Loan/Lending
ESW	Economic and sector work
GTZ	German Agency for Technical Cooperation
IEG	Independent Evaluation Group
IMF	International Monetary Fund
LASED	Land Allocation for Social and Economic Development (Cambodia)
NGO	Nongovernmental organization
OP	Operational Policy
OPCS	Operations Policy and Country Services
PREM	Poverty Reduction and Economic Management Network
PRSP	Poverty Reduction Strategy Paper
PSIA	Poverty and Social Impact Analysis
SAM	Social Accounting Matrix
SDN	Sustainable Development Network

Children with their mothers in Bhutan. Photo by Curt Carnemark, courtesy of the World Bank Photo Library.

Acknowledgments

This report was prepared by a team led by Soniya Carvalho. The core team included Joan Nelson, Manuel Penalver, and Morgan Rota. Catherine Gwin conducted interviews with senior Bank staff and managers, and Shonar Lala interviewed in-country stakeholders and Bank task managers and task team members. Country case reviews were undertaken by Jeffrey Alwang, Jaimie Bleck, Anthony Killick, Shonar Lala, Anne Pitcher, Sylvia Saborio, and Jan Kees van Donge. Jabesh Amissah-Arthur, Happy Kayuni, and David Korboe contributed to the country case reviews. Domenico Lombardi reviewed donor collaboration in Poverty and Social Impact Analyses. Danielle Resnik and Morgan Rota undertook the portfolio review, and Melvin Vaz contributed to it. Antine Legrand and Shampa Sinha contributed to other background work. Pedro Alba, Jeffery Hammer, and Howard White were peer reviewers. Victoria Elliott provided comments. William Hurlbut edited the report and provided document production support. Heather Dittbrenner edited the report for publication. The team was assisted by Romayne Pereira. Juicy Zareen Qureishi-Huq provided administrative and production support. Financial support from the Norwegian Agency for International Development (Norad) is gratefully acknowledged.

The report was initiated under the direction of Alain Barbu, former Manager, Sector Evaluations, and completed under the direction of Monika Huppi, Manager, Sector Evaluations, Independent Evaluation Group.

Director-General, Evaluation: *Vinod Thomas*
Director, Independent Evaluation Group – World Bank: *Cheryl Gray*
Manager, Independent Evaluation Group, Sector Evaluations: *Monika Huppi*
Task Manager: *Soniya Carvalho*

Boys in Nigeria. Photo by Curt Carnemark, courtesy of the World Bank Photo Library.

Foreword

The current global financial and economic crises are likely to put enormous pressure on governments to respond with immediate measures and to undertake far-reaching reforms in the medium term, requiring a substantial increase in donor support. To protect the poor and enhance benefits to them, key policy reforms will need to be underpinned by systematic analysis of their expected poverty and social impacts. The World Bank's experience to date with the Poverty and Social Impact Analysis (PSIA) approach provides useful lessons for addressing these issues.

Introduced in fiscal 2002, the PSIA approach aimed to help the Bank and its client countries understand the distributional impacts of policy reforms and design reform processes that took account of beneficiaries and those adversely affected. The PSIA approach was also expected to provide an understanding of the institutional and political constraints to development and help build domestic ownership of policy reforms.

The World Bank had already been conducting distributional analyses before the introduction of the PSIA approach. However, this approach was distinctive in emphasizing the use of social and economic analytical tools and techniques to conduct ex ante analysis of the impacts of economywide policy reforms and in supporting a more systematic use of that analysis to inform policy advice and design. By fiscal 2007 the Bank had undertaken 156 pieces of analytical work using one or more elements of the PSIA approach in 75 countries across several sectors. Total Bank and other donor support to PSIAs was $15 million from fiscal 2004 to fiscal 2006.

Consistent with the roles envisaged by the Bank for PSIAs, this study distils three operational objectives for evaluation: the effect of PSIAs on country policies, their contribution to country analytic capacity, and their effect on Bank operations. This study finds that PSIAs have had a moderate effect on country policies and Bank operations and a negligible effect on country analytic capacity, on average, although there have been some outstanding examples of success.

Overall, implementation of the PSIA approach has had considerable limitations. There have been tensions between the various operational objectives assigned to PSIAs. The tensions concern inconsistencies between informing country and Bank policy decisions in a timely way and building country analytic capacity. PSIAs have had limited ownership by Bank staff and managers and have often not been effectively integrated into country assistance programs. Quality assurance, monitoring, and evaluation of the overall effectiveness of PSIAs have been weak.

To improve PSIAs' effectiveness, this evaluation recommends that the Bank take measures to ensure that staff fully understand what the PSIA approach is and when to use it, clarify the operational objectives of each PSIA, and ensure that the approach and timeline adopted are aligned with those objectives. Quality assurance mechanisms should be strengthened to ensure that PSIAs are designed to achieve the intended effects. The evaluation also recommends that the Bank shift significant decision-making and funding authority for PSIAs to the Regional Vice Presidencies and ensure that PSIAs are grounded in country assistance programs.

Vinod Thomas

Student at the public primary school in Tegucigalpa, Honduras. Photo by Alfredo Srur, courtesy of the World Bank Photo Library.

Executive Summary

The World Bank introduced the Poverty and Social Impact Analysis (PSIA) approach in fiscal 2002 to help governments and the Bank anticipate and address the possible consequences of proposed policy reforms, especially on the poor and vulnerable, and to contribute to country capacity for policy analysis. By fiscal 2007 the Bank had undertaken 156 pieces of analytical work using one or more elements of the PSIA approach (hereafter called PSIAs) in 75 countries and 14 sectors. Total donor support to PSIAs over fiscal 2004–06 was $15 million, which came from the Bank's earmarked Incremental Fund for PSIAs ($5.8 million), earmarked PSIA Trust Funds contributed by various bilateral donors, and non-earmarked Bank budget and other donor funding.

The Bank had been conducting distributional analysis in some of its economic and sector work even before the introduction of PSIAs. As early as 1987 the Bank's Operational Guidelines required analysis of the short-term impact of adjustment programs on the urban and rural poor. The PSIA approach was distinctive in emphasizing the use of social and economic analytical tools and techniques to conduct ex ante analysis of the impacts of economywide policy reforms and more systematic use of that analysis to inform policy advice and design.

Development literature has emphasized the importance of understanding the institutional and political constraints to development, building domestic ownership of policy reforms, and assessing the distributional impacts of policy actions. The PSIA approach correctly emphasizes these aspects. The Bank has produced a substantial body of guidance on how to address these aspects, and that guidance has been refined over time to incorporate lessons learned.

This evaluation finds that although there have been some highly effective individual PSIAs, overall implementation of the approach has had considerable limitations, and there are tensions between the various operational objectives assigned to PSIAs. The tensions concern inconsistencies between informing country and Bank policy decisions in a timely way and building country analytic capacity. Furthermore, PSIAs do not always explicitly state the operational objectives related to their intended effect, which reduces the chance that there will be a well-conceived strategy to achieve this effect. PSIAs have had limited ownership by Bank staff and managers and have often not been effectively integrated into country assistance programs. Quality assurance, monitoring, and evaluation of the overall effectiveness of PSIAs have been weak.

To improve PSIA effectiveness, the evaluation recommends that the Bank take measures to ensure that staff fully understand what the PSIA approach is and when to use it, clarify the operational objectives of each PSIA, and ensure that the approach and timeline adopted are aligned with those objectives. Quality assurance mechanisms should be strengthened to ensure that PSIAs are designed to achieve the intended effects. The evaluation also recommends that the Bank shift significant decision-making and funding authority for PSIAs to the Regional Vice Presidencies and ensure that PSIAs are grounded in country assistance programs.

Introduction

The development community first became concerned about the impacts of economic policy reforms on the poor during the structural adjustment period of the 1980s. In the 1980s and '90s, external groups continuously criticized the International Monetary Fund and the World Bank for failing to properly assess the impacts of the policy reforms they supported. In response, the Bank in fiscal 2002 introduced PSIA. According to the revised Operational Policy (OP 8.60) on development policy lending issued in 2004, Development Policy Loans with likely and significant poverty and social consequences were required to summarize in their program documents relevant analytic knowledge of these consequences. But the Operational Policy does not mandate that the PSIA approach be used to undertake an assessment of these consequences.

The Bank supported 156 PSIAs over fiscal 2002–07, partly driven by the availability of earmarked funds both from within the Bank and from the United Kingdom's Department for International Development, the German Agency for Technical Cooperation, Norway, Italy, Belgium, and Finland. The PSIAs were done mainly in the context of Development Policy Loans, but some

also aimed to inform Country Assistance Strategies, investment loans, and analytical work.

Evaluation Background

Although the Bank has submitted progress reports to donors regarding the implementation of PSIAs, it has not yet completed a comprehensive self-evaluation of the PSIA experience. This evaluation by the Independent Evaluation Group, requested by the Bank's Board of Executive Directors, represents the first independent evaluation of the PSIA experience.

The PSIA experience is highly relevant today. The recent financial crisis and global slowdown are likely to put pressure on governments and donors to undertake far-reaching reforms. To protect the poor and enhance benefits to them, key reforms will need to be underpinned by systematic analysis of their expected poverty and social impacts.

The Bank has envisaged several roles for PSIAs, mainly in the elaboration and implementation of poverty reduction strategies in developing countries, supporting in-country capacity building, and informing Bank operations. These roles can be distilled into three operational objectives that form the basis for the questions addressed in this evaluation:

1. What effect have PSIAs had on country policies (including policy debate)?

Box ES.1: What Is a PSIA?

The Bank defines PSIA as "analysis of the distributional impact of policy reforms on the well-being of different stakeholder groups, with particular focus on the poor and vulnerable."

The Bank sees the innovative aspects of PSIA as "the application of the tools and techniques of social and economic analysis to analyze impacts of economywide policy reforms

before those reforms are carried out (ex ante analysis), and more systematic use of that analysis to inform policy advice and policy design."

The Bank has identified two key elements of PSIA: "First, an analysis to determine the distributional impacts, and second, a process that engages appropriate stakeholders in policy making."

Sources: World Bank (2003h, 2006n, 2008b).

2. What contribution have PSIAs made to the development of country capacity for policy analysis?
3. What effect have PSIAs had on Bank operations (including strategy and analytical work)?

This evaluation covers analytical work identified as PSIAs by the Bank's Poverty Reduction and Economic Management (PREM) and Sustainable Development Network (SDN) Anchors. Analyses not identified as PSIAs by these anchors are not covered.

The two anchors identified 156 analyses as PSIAs over the fiscal 2002–07 period. This evaluation draws its findings from the following resources: a portfolio review of a statistically representative sample of 58 out of the universe of 156 PSIAs; in-depth country case reviews of 12 PSIAs in 8 countries with Regional, sectoral, and fiscal year coverage; and interviews with key informants. This last resource includes interviews with country stakeholders and Bank staff associated with an additional 11 PSIAs in 10 countries and interviews with senior Bank staff and managers.

Main Findings

Objectives
The portfolio review found that about one-fifth of the PSIAs have not explicitly identified which of the three operational objectives they intend to pursue. Among those that have identified operational objectives, informing country policies has been the most frequently stated, followed by informing Bank operations and increasing country capacity for policy analysis. Most PSIAs have had more than one operational objective. About a third of the task manager survey respondents indicated that their PSIA pursued all three objectives.

Pursuit of the multiple operational objectives of PSIAs can create tension and raise unrealistic expectations of what a PSIA can achieve. For example, PSIAs seeking to inform government policy decisions must adjust to the timing of the decision process, but often that is inconsistent

with the approach required to build country analytic capacity.

Content and approach
PSIA practice has frequently departed from the initial guidance on how PSIAs should be conducted. The portfolio review shows the following:

- Even though PSIAs originated out of concern about the impact of reform programs, about one-third of the PSIAs in the portfolio review did not examine well-specified reforms but were more general sector or macroeconomic analyses.
- About one-third of the PSIAs explicitly identified beneficiaries or those adversely affected, and about half did not, although they included disaggregated data or results.
- About 60 percent of the sampled PSIAs identified the institutions responsible for implementing the reform.
- More than half of the sampled PSIAs included some sort of stakeholder participation, but no consultations were mentioned for about two-fifths of the PSIAs.

PSIAs have had widely varying characteristics partly because Bank staff have an unclear understanding of them. At the same time, analytical work possessing PSIA-like characteristics has not always been classified by the Bank as "PSIA." These errors of omission and commission are likely to have inhibited quality assurance and lesson learning.

Effect on country policies
Tracing links between PSIA analyses and country decisions is often difficult, especially where the PSIA is only one of many possible influences. PSIA effects may also be diffuse and occur over time—a report may have no discernable impact on immediate action yet may affect ideas and debate that shape future policy choices. This evaluation focuses only on near-term effects of PSIAs.

The PSIAs reviewed in this evaluation had a moderate effect on country policies, on average, although there have been some outstanding examples of success. Informing a policy process is not easy and requires the convergence of a number of factors. These include the operational focus of the PSIA, a match between PSIA topic and country priorities, government ownership, engagement of parts of the government that have policy jurisdiction over the areas covered by the PSIA, engagement with appropriate nongovernmental stakeholders, timeliness in relation to country decision-making processes, sensitivity to the politics of reform, and active dissemination beyond the distribution of reports. One or a few of these factors have been present in most PSIAs, but the presence of a majority of these factors—which has occurred only in some PSIAs—is important for substantial effect.

Contribution to country capacity

The PSIAs reviewed suggest a negligible contribution to country analytic capacity, on average, with a few positive examples. The main reason for this finding is that most PSIAs have treated this objective as a by-product rather than a core concern, and there has been a tension between the need to provide timely inputs to policy decisions and the longer-term sustained engagement needed to build capacity. Where capacity building has been an explicit objective, it has not always been backed by an appropriate strategy to achieve it. Many PSIAs have involved local ministries, consulting firms, nongovernmental organizations, academics, or local consultants, and others have held training workshops to transfer skills. However, the time allocated to either of these approaches has generally been insufficient to build lasting capacity for policy analysis. The few PSIAs reviewed that have successfully helped build capacity have taken a more deliberate approach. Given that in many—perhaps most—situations, the time frame and approach required for capacity building are inconsistent with the approach needed to inform timely government decision making, greater selectivity in operational objectives is desirable; more effective approaches to building country analytic capacity will also be needed.

Effect on Bank operations

The PSIAs reviewed suggest a moderate effect on Bank operations, on average, with some outstanding examples of success. Key factors that have inhibited PSIA effect on Bank operations include the ambiguity of the PSIA concept; insufficient country director buy-in, resulting in lack of grounding of the PSIA in the country assistance program; and weak engagement between PSIA teams and other operational staff.

Interviews with senior Bank staff and managers indicate that the uptake of PSIAs by country directors and operational teams remains dependent on individual inclinations more than it reflects established practice. There has been only modest acceptance so far of the PSIA as a robust practice across the Bank, although staff directly involved with PSIAs see a number of corporate benefits from the experience, notably the creation of an important body of knowledge through PSIA guidance and an appreciation of the importance of process issues in addition to analytics. However, operational staff lack a common understanding about the objectives and processes of the PSIA approach. PREM Anchor staff generally tend to focus on economic analysis, and SDN staff tend to emphasize mixed methods, including social and institutional analysis and a participatory process.

The 2008 PSIA Good Practice Note (World Bank 2008b) is an improvement over the 2004 PSIA Good Practice Note (World Bank 2004f) in that it helps to lighten PSIA guidance, which was previously seen by staff as overly demanding. The 2008 Note provides Bank staff with the flexibility to determine, based on country context, the balance among economic, social, institutional, and political analyses (and between quantitative and qualitative techniques) and between analytics and such process issues as stakeholder participation and disclosure. The 2008 Note does not, however, require staff to provide a rationale for the particular choices made. Providing a rationale is especially important to ensure that Bank staff from the different networks do not continue to place undue emphasis on their respective disciplinary approaches in undertaking PSIAs.

The PSIA approach has correctly emphasized the importance of understanding the institutional and political constraints to development and the need to build domestic ownership of policy reforms in addition to assessing the distributional impact of policy actions. But implementation of the approach has had considerable limitations. Some notable successes have modeled what PSIAs can accomplish when done right. The recommendations below are intended to help improve PSIA implementation and realize its potential.

Recommendations

This evaluation makes four recommendations to strengthen the Bank's work using the PSIA approach, whether done as freestanding analysis or embedded in other analytical work.

- **Ensure that staff understand what the PSIA approach is and when to use it. Bank management can do this by providing clear guidance (perhaps through updating of the 2008 PSIA Good Practice Note) and actively disseminating this guidance, particularly on—**
  - Whether and how the PSIA approach differs from other distributional analyses, including whether the inclusion of the word "social" in Poverty and Social Impact Analysis suggests the need to include a different type of analysis
  - Whether or not PSIAs should be linked to specific reforms and identify beneficiaries and those adversely affected by the reform
  - What criteria should be used to determine when the PSIA approach is appropriate for a particular operation in a country program.
- **Clarify the operational objectives of each PSIA with regard to its intended effect, and tailor the approach to those objectives, ensuring that the concept note—**
  - Contains a clear statement of the operational objectives of the PSIA with respect to the intended effect (not just the topics/issues to be analyzed)
  - Indicates how its approach—in particular, stakeholder engagement, team composition, partner institutions, budget, and time frame—has been tailored to meet the operational objectives and provides the rationale for the choices made
  - Shows how any tensions and trade-offs among the operational objectives will be reconciled
  - Discusses if the intended dissemination audience and strategy are consistent with the stated operational objectives.
- **Improve integration of the PSIA into the Bank's country assistance program by—**
  - Shifting significant decision-making and funding authority to the Regional Vice Presidencies to ensure that the PSIA topics, scope, and approach are consistent with the country assistance program and that PSIAs ask questions that are relevant to policy
  - Requiring that all earmarked funding for PSIAs be matched by a substantial contribution from the country unit budget.
- **Strengthen PSIA effectiveness through enhanced quality assurance, including—**
  - Subjecting PSIAs to systematic review by Regional management at concept and completion stages to ensure relevance and fit of the PSIA to the country assistance program as well as consistency of the proposed approach with operational objectives, in addition to ensuring technical quality
  - Ensuring that the Bank establishes a monitoring and self-evaluation system designed to assess whether PSIAs are being undertaken where appropriate and are achieving their stated operational objectives.

Two women with grain in Ghana. Photo by Curt Carnemark, courtesy of the World Bank Photo Library.

Management Response

Introduction

Management regards the Independent Evaluation Group (IEG) review of the World Bank's Poverty and Social Impact Analysis (PSIA) as a comprehensive attempt to reflect lessons from a wide range of PSIA done by the Bank. The findings of the review reflect work conducted through a mix of portfolio review and interviews and highlight important areas where the PSIA approach can be strengthened.

Support for Strengthening the PSIA Process. The emphasis of the report in the following areas is especially welcome: the need to specify clear operational objectives; the importance of political economy in doing poverty and distributional analysis; the need for strong linkages between the country unit and the PSIA team; the potential for more effective use of PSIA findings to inform monitoring and evaluation systems; and the importance of strengthening quality assurance. Although robust progress has been made on many of these crucial elements, IEG's observations will assist future actions in these areas.

A Differing View on Some Elements. That said, management is of the view that some of the findings of the report are based on a partial understanding of the PSIA approach, including its objectives and limitations. The comments below on the analysis in the review reflect this differing view. Management broadly concurs with IEG's recommendations on the way forward to enhance the effectiveness of PSIA and notes a number of actions already taken or planned in the directions suggested by the recommendations.

Management's Views on the Findings

Management concurs with much of the analysis but believes that the analytical framework makes some of the finding ambiguous. It also notes an issue that is often difficult in evaluation—the fact that approaches like PSIA evolve continually based on experience. That said, management is in broad agreement with the thrust of the recommendations.

A Flexible Approach. Some of the key findings of the evaluation appear to be linked to its treatment of PSIA as more of a standardized approach adhering to somewhat rigid guidelines, rather than one that incorporates a range of tools and methods to be flexibly applied to specific situations.[1] As reflected in the initial PSIA User's Guide, the revised Good Practice Note, and the forthcoming revised PREM-SDV Web page, PSIA comprises a range of tools that can be applied to analyze distributional and social impacts in widely varying situations, depending on the specific contexts of policy reform and country circumstances. The updated Good Practice Note of 2008 reinforces the flexible nature of the approach as necessary for PSIA to be effective in informing policy dialogue and operations. In particular, the evaluation of PSIA against the three specific criteria selected by IEG (see below) appears to flow from IEG's treatment of PSIA as a standardized approach.

Criteria for Evaluating PSIA Work. Some of the findings of the review appear to be based on criteria drawn from an overly broad characterization of the objectives of PSIA. Based on the Good Practice Note, the institution defines the main objective of the PSIA approach to be to analyze the distributional impact of policy reforms on the well-being or welfare of different groups, with particular focus on the poor and vulnerable. The review, on the other hand, uses what IEG considers as PSIA's three goals from its reading of PSIA documents as the criteria for evaluation—effect on country policies, supporting in-country capacity building, and informing Bank operations—without making the distinction between the main objective and potential benefits. Informing country policies and building capacity in countries should be considered as desirable second-order impacts that may come from a process of engagement over time, but rarely from a single PSIA exercise.

Evolution of PSIA over Time. The review takes a somewhat static view of PSIA, which in management's view does not adequately reflect the significant progress made over the last seven years. The learning and evolution over time has resulted in the refinement of the institutional understanding and guidance concerning best practice of PSIA, which has been reflected in the Good Practice Note of 2008. The static view adopted by the review also gives little indication of whether some of the problems highlighted in the evaluation were mitigated over time.[2] This, in management's view, constitutes a missed opportunity to draw lessons for the future, by identifying and analyzing areas where progress has been made and where it has been harder to achieve.

Recommendations

As noted above, management concurs with the broad thrust of IEG's recommendations and will undertake actions to address the issues raised. Management's specific responses to IEG recommendations are given in the Management Action Record matrix.

Better Integration into Bank Programs. Management concurs with IEG's recommendations to ensure better integration of PSIA into the Bank's program and enhance the quality assurance process of PSIA. Conclusions along similar lines are emerging from internal reviews of PSIA by PREM and SDV anchor units. A new Multi-Donor Trust Fund to support PSIA work, to be operational in fiscal 2010, incorporates a number of features consistent with these recommendations. The Trust Fund assigns responsibility to the Regions, in terms of allocating funds, monitoring, and quality review of the analytical work funded by the Trust Fund.

Guidance. Management concurs with the recommendation to provide clear guidance to Bank staff about what the PSIA approach involves and when it can be used. Over the years, a number of knowledge products on PSIA have been developed and updated, including comprehensive user guides, Good Practice Notes, methodological notes, and edited volumes. The outreach of such materials will be enhanced further through an improved Web site and more frequent and accessible learning events, drawing on additional resources provided by the aforementioned Multi-Donor Trust Fund. Management, however, notes an important caveat in addressing this recommendation. Efforts to expand awareness about the PSIA approach must be careful to not create perceptions of minimum or universal standards for PSIA, and instead stress the flexibility of the approach to adapt to specific country and policy contexts.

Management Action Record

IEG recommendation	Management response
Ensure that staff understand what the PSIA approach is and when to use it by providing clear guidance (perhaps through updating of the 2008 PSIA Good Practice Note) disseminated to staff and disseminating this guidance, particularly on— • Whether and how the PSIA approach differs from other distributional analyses, including whether the inclusion of the word "social" in Poverty and Social Impact Analysis suggests the need to include a different type of analysis • Whether or not PSIAs should be linked to specific reforms and identify beneficiaries and those adversely affected by the reform • What criteria should be used to determine when the PSIA approach is appropriate for a particular operation in a country program.	**Agreed.** Management agrees that it should disseminate more widely what is meant by the PSIA approach as outlined in the 2008 Good Practice Note. Management, however, notes an important caveat in addressing this recommendation. Efforts to expand awareness about the PSIA approach must be careful to not create perceptions of minimum or universal standards for PSIA, and instead stress the flexibility of the approach to adapt to specific country and policy contexts. The revised Good Practice Note (GPN) discusses key elements of the PSIA approach: first, an analysis to determine the distributional impacts and, second, a process that engages appropriate stakeholders in policy making.[3] The GPN also makes it clear that an ideal PSIA will vary based on country and reform-specific conditions. In particular, the range and extent of stakeholder engagement in the PSIA process will vary according to the political context of the reform and the related opportunities for promoting the public debate on policy options. The GPN clarifies when it could be a priority for a country team to carry out detailed PSIA: when there are potential negative poverty and social impacts on different groups, particularly poor and vulnerable groups; when there is potential to significantly improve the benefits of a reform for poor and vulnerable groups; the prominence and urgency of the report in the government's policy agenda; and the level of debate surrounding the reform. With regard to the methods and tools adopted for PSIA, the GPN stresses the need for flexibility as well. While multidisciplinary or mixed methods of analysis enhance the understanding of the poverty and social impacts of a reform, the design of the methodology and the selection of tools will depend on the nature of the reform problem being addressed, the availability and quality of data, the time available for analysis, and the available in-country capacity. PREM and SDV are already incorporating the revised GPN into their PSIA-related learning programs (Fundamentals of Bank Operations, PSIA e-learning, PSIA course). Management will further enhance outreach using these materials through an improved Web site that more clearly frames the main objective and potential benefits, as well as the need for a flexible approach, and more frequent and accessible learning events, drawing on additional resources provided by the aforementioned Multi-Donor Trust Fund. Management will consider its agreed action complete with the full roll-out of these activities in fiscal 2010.
Clarify the operational objectives of each PSIA with regard to its intended effect and tailor the approach to those objectives, ensuring that the concept note— • Contains a clear statement of the operational objectives of the PSIA with respect to the intended effect (not just the topics/issues to be analyzed) • Indicates how its approach—in particular stakeholder engagement, team composition, partner institutions, budget, and time frame—has been tailored to meet the operational objectives, and provides the rationale for the choices made • Shows how any tensions and trade-offs among the operational objectives will be reconciled • Discusses if the intended dissemination audience and strategy are consistent with the stated operational objectives.	**Agreed.** Management agrees that poverty, social, and distributional impact analysis should have a clear operational objective and a methodology and strategy for stakeholder engagement and dissemination that is consistent with the operational objective. Almost all PSIA type analysis is done in the context of economic and sector work (ESW), where Bank guidelines require that the operational objective, scope, and participatory approaches be clearly specified in the concept note. The revised GPN indicates that poverty, social, and distributional analysis should be an integral part of the ESW cycle. All dissemination activities need to be fully consistent with the Bank's Disclosure Policy. PSIA can also be done in the context of technical assistance, where the objective is to strengthen client institutions and capacity to influence reforms or as a factual technical document analyzing a specific policy reform supported by a Development Policy Operation. Once operational, the new PSIA trust fund will require that the Regions detail in their concept notes how they will ensure that poverty, social, and distributional analysis (supported by the Trust Fund) is treated as an ESW, technical assistance, or a project-related factual technical document. Management will consider its agreed action complete with the introduction of these requirements.

(*continued on next page*)

Management Action Record

IEG recommendation	Management response
Improve integration of the PSIA into the Bank's country assistance program by— • Shifting decision-making and funding authority to the Regional Vice Presidencies to ensure that the PSIA topics, scope, and approach are consistent with the country assistance program and that PSIAs ask policy-relevant questions • Requiring that all earmarked funding for PSIAs be matched by a substantial contribution from the country unit budget.	**Agreed.** Poverty, social, and distributional impact analysis that is part of ESW, technical assistance, or a project-related factual technical document is currently managed and funded by the Regions. The revised GPN explicitly advises that poverty, social, and distributional impact analysis be anchored in the Country Assistance Strategy (CAS). Under the revised policy for poverty reduction (OP 1.00), the CAS summarizes existing knowledge on poverty, identifies analytical gaps, and presents the work program by the Bank and others to fill these gaps. The CAS can usefully lay out key reform areas that the Bank will support and indicate whether there are any plans for poverty, social, and distributional impact analysis. The new PSIA trust fund will decentralize the management of resources for poverty, social, and distributional impact analysis carried out as ESW, technical assistance, and factual technical documents to the Regions. The Regions will be required to provide matching resources from the country unit budget. The annual Trust Fund Regional monitoring reports will indicate the share of matching resources provided to complement Trust Fund support. Management will consider its agreed actions complete with the roll-out of the trust fund.
Strengthen PSIA effectiveness through enhanced quality assurance, including— • Subjecting PSIAs to systematic review by Regional management at the concept and completion stages to ensure relevance and fit of the PSIA to the country assistance program as well as consistency of the proposed approach with operational objectives, in addition to ensuring technical quality • Ensuring that the Bank establishes a monitoring and self-evaluation system designed to assess whether PSIAs are being undertaken where appropriate and are achieving their stated operational objectives.	**Agreed.** PSIA work that is part of ESW is subject to Regional quality assurance procedures and the preparation of an activity completion report. As noted in the Management Response to IEG's evaluation of ESW and technical assistance, management will undertake a review of analytic and advisory activities in fiscal 2010 that will address institutional arrangements, notably quality assurance. The quality and effectiveness of PSIA informing the Bank's Development Policy Operations has been monitored through the retrospective assessment of the Bank's Development Policy Lending portfolio that has been carried out every two years by Operations Policy and Country Services. A Development Policy Operation retrospective is under preparation and will be available early in fiscal 2010. The proposed PSIA trust fund annual Regional monitoring reports as well as the final independent Trust Fund evaluation will assess the extent to which poverty, social, and distributional analysis (supported by the Trust Fund) has met its operational objectives and has had an impact on the ground. Management will consider its agreed actions complete with the completion of the fiscal 2010 analytic and advisory activities review and the implementation of changes coming out of that process, the issuance of the Development Policy Operation retrospective, and the implementation of the trust fund reporting system.

Chairperson's Summary: Committee on Development Effectiveness (CODE)

On June 3, 2009, the Committee on Development Effectiveness (CODE) met to consider the document *How Effective Have Poverty and Social Impact Analyses Been? An IEG Study of World Bank Support to PSIAs,* prepared by the Independent Evaluation Group (IEG), together with the draft management response.

Overall Conclusions. The Committee welcomed the timely discussion of IEG's study of Poverty and Social Impact Analysis (PSIA), particularly in light of the ongoing discussion to establish a Multi-Donor Trust Fund to support PSIA work, to be operational in fiscal 2010. Members recommended enhancing the use of PSIA but clarifying the operational objectives of each PSIA exercise. They proposed establishing a hierarchy of objectives and following up on PSIA findings with appropriate dissemination and disclosure, including in several languages. They stressed the importance of linkage with country assistance programs and flexibility in PSIA, albeit with clear accountability, rather than having a standardized approach adhering to rigid guidelines. There were comments on the importance of capacity building but perhaps as a second-order objective of PSIA. Members felt that important lessons could be drawn from the past experience in conducting PSIA. In this regard, they felt the decentralized management of the new PSIA Trust Fund to the Regions was appropriate. The desirability for the Bank to share the PSIA report with other donors or development partners was mentioned.

The following key issues were raised at the meeting:

PSIA Operational Objectives. Many members stressed the importance of PSIA in emphasizing social and economic analysis ex ante on the distributional impact of policy reform, with particular focus on the poor. They agreed that the operational objectives of such analysis should be clarified and adapted to each specific country policy context. Some members underlined that PSIA should not be an item within a checklist to be complied with once an intervention has already been decided, and suggested that poverty distribution analysis ideally should be conducted upstream so as to be an input to policy design. There were comments on the relevance of the objectives of informing the country policies and building capacity in client countries to conduct their own PSIA. However, there were also views that perhaps both should be second-order objectives of PSIA. One member felt that building capacity should not be an objective at all because it requires separate activities. One speaker queried whether local institutions could be more involved in the preparation of PSIA.

Questions were raised on integration and compliance with Operational Policy 8.60, which requires that the Bank determine whether specific country policies supported by Development Policy Loans (DPLs) are likely to have significant poverty and social impact. Supporting assessment can be done through PSIA or embedded in other analytic work. In addition, there were questions on the rationale and criteria for country selection, and who initiates the request or proposal for conducting a PSIA. One member asked to what extent gender issues have been adequately mainstreamed in the new Good Practice Note. *Management agreed with IEG on the need to ensure that staff understand what the PSIA approach is and stated that it would disseminate widely the revised Good Practice Note, and enhance the quality assurance process.*

Country Program. Speakers underscored the need for PSIA to become an integral part of country assistance programs and Bank operations, and to consider the political economy dimension in doing poverty and distribution analysis. The need for stronger linkages between country units and PSIA teams was emphasized. Some speakers noted the need for flexibility in applying a range of tools and methods to specific situations rather than treating PSIA as a standardized approach. It was also suggested that the topic and timing of the PSIA should be aligned with the country's priorities and the objectives of the Country Assistance Strategy (CAS). Relatedly, there were comments on the need for engaging country stakeholders to build ownership, especially among policy makers. There were also questions on the extent to which PSIAs are used in the design of DPLs. In addition, some members sought further information on countries' demand for PSIA. *Management agreed with IEG's recommendation on the need to ensure better integration of PSIA into the Bank's country program. Management clarified that a number of issues, including compliance with Operational Policy 8.60 and consultations with stakeholders, will be addressed in the DPL Retrospective report currently under preparation.*

Knowledge. Some members felt that in the context of the knowledge agenda there was extensive experience that should be used to better implement the PSIA approach in the future. In this regard, they encouraged more dissemination, including translation into local languages and follow-up of PSIA findings. One member felt that in addition to an analysis ex ante on the distributional impact of policy reform, ex post evaluations would be valuable contributions to knowledge. Some questions were raised on PSIA's relationship with economic and sector work, including Poverty Assessments. *Management stated that PSIA is a set of tools that are frequently conducted in the context of DPLs and often used in Poverty Assessments, Public Expenditure Review, and other core economic and sector work or in the preparation of investment projects. It also clarified that regional PSIA teams draw on staff from all networks and Development Economics and the Chief Economist and are further supported by the Poverty Reduction and Economic Management and Sustainable Development Anchors. It also noted that it is working to enhance the outreach of knowledge in PSIA and to improve Web-based learning. IEG pointed out that there is still insufficient ownership of PSIA findings by operational staff and managers within the Bank.*

Trust Fund. Some members felt that the main purpose of the Trust Fund should not be to save resources from regular budget. They also proposed the new Trust Fund should be designed to finance activities in which PSIA was not regularly used. A question was raised on possible lack of sustainability of PSIA funded through earmarked Multi-Donor Trust Funds. There was also a request for the Bank to share the findings of PSIA with other donors. Relatedly, a comment was raised on the need to understand whether important donor-funded activities are not bought by country directors, who therefore do not integrate them in CASs. The recommendation on shifting the decision-making and funding mandate of the new Trust Fund to Regional vice presidential units was welcomed. *Management clarified that the bulk of resources used to support PSIA comes from Bank resources, and that the financial contributions from the new Trust Fund will be very small. However, it indicated that it hopes to leverage the new Trust Fund so as to make the Regional vice presidential units more responsible and accountable for carrying out this analysis.*

Monitoring and Evaluation (M&E). Some members took note that about 75 percent of the sample PSIA did not include M&E indicators or data collection methods necessary for monitoring the impact of reform policy. They underscored the potential for more effective use of PSIA findings to inform the M&E systems.

Giovanni Majnoni, Chairperson

Chapter 1

Evaluation Highlights

- The World Bank has defined Poverty and Social Impact Analysis (PSIA) as "the analysis of the distributional impact of policy reforms on the well-being of different stakeholder groups, with particular focus on the poor and vulnerable."
- PSIAs were a donor response to the concerns of external groups—not client countries—about the impact of Bank-supported programs and policies.
- A Bank Operational Policy requires Development Policy Loans with likely significant poverty and social impacts to address those impacts, but there is no specific requirement to do so using the PSIA approach.
- The Bank has supported 156 PSIAs, partly driven by the availability of earmarked funds both from within the Bank and from other donors.
- Consistent with the roles envisaged by the World Bank for PSIAs, this evaluation assesses their effect on country policies and Bank operations and their contribution to country analytic capacity.

Hanoi, Vietnam, bicycle and scooter riders. Photo by Simone D. McCourtie, courtesy of the World Bank Photo Library.

Introduction

Countries—both their governments and the public—need to understand the probable distributional impact of policy reforms and programs. Equipped with that information, they need to design reform processes that take account of beneficiaries and those adversely affected, if they are going to be effective in achieving objectives of growth and poverty reduction. Experience has shown that understanding and defining effective reform processes often require careful economic and social analyses of the potential impacts of the reforms within specific country contexts.

In fiscal 2002, the World Bank introduced a distinctive analytical approach—the Poverty and Social Impact Analysis (PSIA)—to help countries achieve this kind of evidence-based policy making and to ensure that its own operations take distributional impacts into account. This evaluation assesses the effect of Bank-supported analytical work that uses one or more elements of the PSIA approach (hereafter called PSIAs) both on the countries and on the Bank itself from fiscal 2002 to 2007.

The impetus to assess the poverty and social impacts of World Bank operations can be traced back to the mid-1990s, when external groups criticized the International Monetary Fund (IMF) and the World Bank for not properly assessing the impacts of reforms before supporting them. In the late 1990s, several steps were taken to improve the poverty reduction focus of Bank operations; among these steps was the development of the poverty reduction strategy process.

This process was designed to ensure that reforms were aligned with the domestic priorities of client countries (Wolfenson 1997). As stated in a World Bank publication, "Following the adoption of the [poverty reduction strategy] approach, the World Bank and International Monetary Fund committed, in 2001, to a systematic assessment of the poverty and social impacts of policy reforms" (World Bank 2006n).

The Bank had been conducting distributional analysis in some of its economic and sector work (ESW) even before the introduction of PSIAs. In fact, as early as 1987 the Bank's Operational Guidelines required an analysis of the short-term impact of adjustment programs on the urban and rural poor (World Bank 1987). Then, over the 1987–92 period, the World Bank, the African Development Bank, and the United Nations Development Programme jointly supported the Social Dimensions of Adjustment in Africa

Three main roles were envisaged for PSIAs—the elaboration and implementation of poverty reduction strategies in developing countries, supporting in-country capacity building, and informing Bank operations.

Program, which aimed to help participating African countries integrate poverty and social concerns in the design and implementation of their adjustment programs. And in 1996, in conjunction with national governments and civil society organizations, the World Bank launched the Structural Adjustment Participatory Review Initiative to assess the economic and social impact of structural adjustment policies on various social groups in borrowing countries.[1] In 2000, a group of nongovernmental organizations (NGOs), led by Oxfam, reminded the Bank of its commitment to assess proposed reforms in Bank programs (Oxfam International 2000). The Bank responded by introducing the PSIA approach in fiscal 2002 as a formal way to conduct distributional analysis. The approach was based on collaborative work with the IMF, the United Kingdom's Department for International Development (DFID), the German Agency for Technical Cooperation (GTZ), and other donors. Appendix A shows the timeline of PSIA history.

What Is a PSIA?

The Bank defines PSIA as "the analysis of the distributional impact of policy reforms on the well-being of different stakeholder groups, with particular focus on the poor and vulnerable" (World Bank 2003g). The Bank laid out 10 key elements of a PSIA in 2003 (see box 1.1) (World Bank 2003h). The Bank sees the distinctive aspects of PSIA as follows: "What is new is the application of the tools and techniques of social and economic analysis to analyze impacts of economy-wide policy reforms before those reforms are carried out (ex ante analysis), and more systematic use of that analysis to inform policy advice and policy design" (World Bank 2006n). Furthermore, the Bank has identified two key elements of the PSIA: "first, an analysis to determine the distributional impacts, and second, a process that engages appropriate stakeholders in policy-making" (World Bank 2008e).

The PSIA approach emphasizes the importance of understanding the institutional and political constraints to development and the need to build domestic ownership of policy reforms in addition to assessing the distributional impact of policy actions.

The Bank has envisaged three main roles for PSIAs: supporting the elaboration and implementation of poverty reduction strategies in developing countries, supporting in-country capacity building, and informing Bank operations (World Bank 2003h, 2004f, 2008e). These roles have been distilled into three operational objectives in this evaluation: informing country policies, contributing to country analytic capacity, and informing Bank operations.

Literature on development over the past decade has emphasized the importance of understanding the institutional and political constraints to development and the need to build domestic ownership of policy reforms in addition to assessing the distributional impact of policy actions. The PSIA approach correctly emphasizes these aspects. As discussed in chapters 2–4, however, implementation of the approach has faced considerable limitations. These include, for example, limited success in fostering a common understanding among Bank staff about what a PSIA is and if and how it differs from other distributional analyses and tensions between being able to inform country and Bank policy decisions in a timely manner and building a country's analytic capacity. Although informing a policy process is not easy and requires several factors to come together (chapter 3), limitations in implementing the PSIA approach have reduced the effectiveness of the approach.

Recent Status

Through fiscal 2007 the Bank funded 156 PSIAs (not including the initial pilot PSIAs), as identified by the Bank's Poverty Reduction and Economic Management (PREM) and Sustainable Development Network (SDN) Anchors. Appendix B provides a list of the 156 PSIAs.[2] Total donor support to PSIAs over fiscal 2004–06 was $15 million, and this funding was partly a driver of PSIAs. It came from the Bank's earmarked Incremental Fund for PSIAs ($5.8 million), earmarked PSIA Trust Funds contributed by various bilateral donors (including DFID, GTZ, Norway, Italy, Belgium, and Finland), and non-earmarked Bank budget and other donor funding. After the exhaustion of the Incremental

Box 1.1: World Bank Guidance on PSIA

The Bank's 2003 PSIA User's Guide (World Bank 2003h) does not specify minimum standards for PSIA; instead it provides suggestions on how to approach the analysis based on 10 key elements. It points out that although there is a logical sequence to these elements, that does not imply that they need to be undertaken in strict order or that all the steps will be feasible in every country.

1. Asking the right questions: Asking questions such as the prominence of the issue on the government's agenda, the timing of the reform, and the nature of the national debate on the issue will help orient the analysis correctly.

2. Identifying stakeholders: An early identification of relevant stakeholders is important. Not only can policy choices affect different stakeholders or economic agents in different ways, but these stakeholders can also influence whether a policy is adopted and how it is implemented.

3. Understanding transmission channels: Once stakeholders have been identified, an important step in the PSIA process is to delineate the channels by which the analyst expects a particular policy change to impact various stakeholder groups.

4. Assessing institutions: An analysis of the market structure and implementing agencies can elucidate what impact policies will have on the welfare of different households or groups.

5. Gathering data and information: Assessing data needs and available data and planning the phasing of future data collection efforts are an important part of PSIA.

6. Analyzing impacts: The choice of tools (such as participatory poverty assessment, benefit incidence analysis, social accounting matrix, or computable general equilibrium) will depend on the expected nature of the impact and the availability of data.

7. Contemplating enhancement and compensation measures: To the extent that there are those who may not benefit from the reform, PSIA can inform policy design, leading to choices that minimize the number of people who are affected negatively or the extent of adverse impacts.

8. Assessing risks: Risk analysis addresses the issue of what could go wrong to prevent policy reform from delivering the intended poverty or social impacts. By addressing these questions explicitly, adjustments can be made to the reform to mitigate the risks.

9. Monitoring and evaluating impacts: Good PSIA calls for monitoring and evaluation, both to validate ex ante analyses and to influence the reformulation of policy.

10. Fostering policy debate and feeding back into policy choice: Fostering and drawing on public discussion of policy can be useful at various points of the PSIA process—for example, to help identify stakeholders and their positions, to understand transmission channels, to validate technical impact analysis, or to leverage social accountability. It is critical for PSIA to ensure that the lessons learned from impact analysis, monitoring and evaluation, social accountability, and public policy debate actually inform and affect policy.

The Bank reinforced these 10 key elements in its 2004 Good Practice Note on PSIA.

Sources: World Bank (2003h, 2004f).

Fund for PSIAs in fiscal 2006, PSIAs were funded from the remaining PSIA Trust Fund resources and Bank budget. The amount of the Bank budget spent on PSIAs after exhaustion of the Incremental Fund is not available.

With the publication of the Bank's revised Operational Policy (OP) on Development Policy Lending (OP 8.60) in 2004, the analysis of poverty and social impacts of development policy lending was made a required part of Bank Development Policy Loans (DPLs) that were likely to have significant poverty and social consequences (box 1.2). However, the extent and nature of this analysis is not specified in the OP itself, although an endnote in the policy refers staff to the accompanying Good Practice Note on Poverty and Social Impact Analysis and Development Policy Lending for guidance on conducting PSIA (World Bank 2004f). Whereas OP 8.60 applies only to DPLs, the Bank has undertaken PSIAs in a range of other contexts, including informing investment projects, Country Assistance Strategies, and

The Bank and other donors funded 156 PSIAs over fiscal 2002–07.

Donor support for PSIAs has amounted to $15 million over fiscal 2004–06 and has included a mix of earmarked Bank funds, earmarked donor funds, and non-earmarked Bank funds.

other analytical work. Most of the PSIAs have, however, been intended to inform DPLs.

Because no Bank OP governs PSIAs, the main sources of guidance for conducting them are the Bank's PSIA User's Guide (World Bank 2003h); some other guidance such as the toolkit for evaluating the poverty and distributional impact of economic policies (World Bank 2003g); a lessons and examples book (World Bank 2006n); practitioners' guides (World Bank 2005a, 2006b); a sourcebook of tools for institutional, political, and social analysis of policy reform (World Bank 2007g); the Good Practice Notes on PSIA (World Bank 2004f, 2008b); and *The Impact of Macro-Economic Policies on Poverty and Income Distribution: Macro-Micro Evaluation Techniques and Tools* (World Bank 2008c). These documents indicate what the Bank expected PSIAs to look like around the time of their initiation and the subsequent evolution in thinking about PSIAs.

OP 8.60 requires that the poverty and social impacts of DPLs that are likely to have significant poverty and social consequences be assessed, but it does not require that this be done through PSIAs.

Responsibility for the promotion of PSIA within the World Bank lies principally with the PREM and SDN Anchors. They have administered the dedicated Incremental Fund for PSIAs and produced the PSIA User's Guide and

sourcebook (World Bank 2003h, 2007g), and, in consultation with the Operational Policy and Country Services (OPCS) Vice Presidential Unit, the PSIA Good Practice Notes (World Bank 2004f, 2008b).

Evaluation Objectives and Rationale

This evaluation responds to a request from the World Bank's Board of Executive Directors for an independent assessment of PSIAs, against the backdrop of the concerns expressed by Oxfam and other NGOs[3] about the effectiveness of PSIA to date and the interest of IDA-15 deputies in strengthening poverty and social impact assessments.[4]

Though the Bank has prepared several progress reports on PSIAs, it has yet to complete a comprehensive self-evaluation of the PSIA experience. Progress reports have been undertaken mainly in the context of reporting back to donors on implementation. There are currently two ongoing reviews of poverty and social impact analysis in the Bank's DPLs—a stocktaking by PREM and a DPL retrospective by OPCS. An ongoing joint Overseas Development Institute and World Bank report on PSIAs (ODI and World Bank 2009) aims to improve the practice and enhance the use of poverty and social impact analysis in the Bank and in partner countries.[5]

Interest in the PSIA experience is likely to increase worldwide. The recent financial crisis

---

Box 1.2: Institutional Requirement Contained in Operational Policy 8.60 Relating to Assessing Poverty and Social Consequences of Reforms

The Bank determines whether specific country policies supported by a DPL are likely to have significant poverty and social consequences, especially for poor people and vulnerable groups. For country policies with likely significant effects, the Bank's program document summarizes relevant analytic knowledge of these effects and of the borrower's systems for reducing adverse effects and enhancing positive effects associated with the specific policies being supported. If there are significant gaps in the analysis or shortcomings in the borrower's systems, the Bank's program document describes how such gaps or shortcomings would be addressed before or during program implementation, as appropriate. OP 8.60 refers staff to a 2004 Good Practice Note on Poverty and Social Impact Analysis (World Bank 2004f) for applying this guidance, including possible criteria for the selection of policies for analysis.

Sources: World Bank (2004f, 2004j).

and global slowdown are likely to put pressure on governments to undertake far-reaching reforms in the medium term. To protect the poor and enhance benefits to them, key reforms will need to be underpinned by systematic analysis of their expected poverty and social impacts.

Evaluation Scope, Questions, and Building Blocks

Scope

This evaluation covers analytical work identified as PSIAs by the Bank's PREM and the SDN Anchors. The evaluation does not cover Bank analyses of poverty and social impacts that the anchors did not identify as PSIAs. The anchors identified 156 analyses that incorporated one or more elements of the PSIA approach over the fiscal 2002–07 period. Most of these are freestanding analyses, but some are embedded in the Bank's other ESW. Accordingly, "PSIA" is used in this evaluation to cover analytical work that incorporates one or more elements of the PSIA approach, regardless of whether this analytical work is freestanding or embedded. During the course of this evaluation, some Bank staff pointed to the existence of PSIA-type work that was not on the PREM/SDN list but that should be, and others pointed to PSIAs currently on the list that they believed should not be there.

This evaluation does not aim to assess the downstream poverty reduction impacts of PSIAs. The attribution problems involved in doing so would be prohibitive. Nor does the evaluation aim to assess compliance with OP 8.60, which is being done by PREM and by OPCS.

Moreover, this evaluation focuses on near-term effects of PSIAs. Longer-term effects can be difficult to trace and are unlikely to be measurable yet for recent PSIAs. However, the evaluation recognizes that a seemingly ineffective PSIA can be powerfully effective in the future.

Other measurement problems also exist. A government decision may accord with recommendations in a PSIA, but similar recommendations may have come from other sources. It is then difficult to assess the PSIA's contribution. Similar problems of attribution apply to decisions or actions within the Bank. The findings of this evaluation should be interpreted bearing these caveats in mind.

The main sources of guidance on conducting PSIAs are the User's Guide; the sourcebook on tools for institutional, political, and social analysis of policy reform; and the Good Practice Notes.

Evaluation questions

Consistent with the three roles the Bank envisaged for PSIAs, this evaluation distils three operational objectives that form the basis for the questions addressed:

Effect at the country level:

- What effect have PSIAs had on country policies (including policy debate)?
- What contribution have PSIAs made to the development of country capacity for policy analysis?[6]

Effect within the Bank:

- What effect have PSIAs had on Bank operations (including strategy and analytical work)?

The questions this evaluation aims to answer derive from the three roles the Bank has envisioned for PSIAs, also referred to as operational objectives in this evaluation.

Building blocks

Evidence from various sources has been used collectively to formulate the findings:

- A portfolio review of a statistically representative sample of 58 PSIAs chosen randomly from the universe of 156 PSIAs.
- Case reviews for 12 PSIAs in 8 countries (Bangladesh, Cambodia, Ghana, Malawi, Mali, Mozambique, Nicaragua, and Zambia) chosen purposively for diverse regional, sectoral, and fiscal year coverage.
- Semistructured telephone interviews with 47 stakeholders (including government officials, private sector representatives, NGO staff, academics and researchers, officials from donor agencies, and Bank staff) chosen purposively to include stakeholders familiar with the PSIA process. These interviews covered 11 PSIAs in 10 countries (and were additional to the ones covered in the country case reviews).

To date, the Bank has not completed a comprehensive self-evaluation of the PSIA experience.

- Interviews with 30 senior Bank staff and managers (including country directors, advisors, and so forth) chosen purposively to include staff who were knowledgeable about PSIA strategy or who were responsible for overseeing PSIAs.
- A thematic review of donor involvement in PSIAs.

- A literature review, including relevant material from several recent evaluations by the Independent Evaluation Group (IEG).

Appendix C provides a detailed description of each of these sources. Chapter 2 provides an overview of PSIAs.

Chapter 2

Evaluation Highlights

- Bank-supported PSIAs over the fiscal 2002–07 period have had widely varying characteristics.
- In many cases, practice has departed from the initial concept of how PSIA should be conducted.
- A desired characteristic that PSIAs have most frequently adopted has been analysis of risks.
- About one-fifth of the sampled PSIAs did not explicitly state any of the three operational objectives relating to the PSIAs' intended effect, which reduced the chance that there would be a well-conceived strategy to achieve or monitor intended effects.
- Practice has not been institutionalized in a way that ensures monitoring and evaluation of PSIAs, which detracts from lesson learning.

Woman in China carrying a crop in her basket. Photo by Curt Carnemark, courtesy of the World Bank Photo Library.

Overview of PSIAs

This chapter focuses on a statistically significant sample of 58 PSIAs from a universe of 156 Bank-identified PSIAs completed between fiscal 2002 and 2007. It presents an overview of this sample in terms of their number, costs, and operational objectives. It also examines how PSIA practice compares with the Bank's initial concept of how such analysis should be conducted.

Numbers and Costs

The 156 PSIAs covered 75 countries and 14 sectors. As shown in figure 2.1, they were concentrated in the Sub-Saharan Africa Region and in the energy and mining, economic policy, and rural sectors.

Over fiscal 2002–07, the average cost of PSIAs was $148,230—somewhat lower than the average of $178,000 for all Bank ESW over fiscal 2002–06 (IEG 2008; World Bank 2009b). The wide range in PSIAs' costs—from $4,000 to $921, 000—attests to the variety of topics and types of products that are classed as PSIA (as discussed below).

About half of the PSIAs over the period fiscal 2002–07 took less than a year to complete, and about a fifth took more than two years. By comparison, 54 percent of Bank ESW over fiscal 2002–06 took less than a year, and 12 percent took more than two years (IEG 2008; World Bank 2009b).

Objectives

Although PSIAs typically cite their objectives relating to the content of the reform or sector they are analyzing, they do not always state their *operational objectives*, that is, objectives pertaining to the effect that the PSIA intends to have. Explicitly stating operational objectives is important because it enables the PSIA to be specifically designed to achieve those objectives.

PSIAs do not always state their operational objectives.

Among the 58 sampled PSIAs, of those that do explicitly state their operational objectives, the most frequently cited operational objective (in more than two-thirds of the cases) has been to inform country policies and/or debate, followed by to inform Bank operations and then to contribute to country capacity (appendix table F.1). About one-fifth of the PSIAs did not explicitly state any of the three operational objectives. Most PSIAs identified more than one objective. Of the 37 responses received from PSIA task managers, about one-third had all three objectives. Appendix table F.1 shows that there are some differences between what task managers consider PSIA objectives and what the PSIA documentation states as the

About one-third of the PSIAs did not examine a well-specified reform but were more general sector or macro-economic analyses.

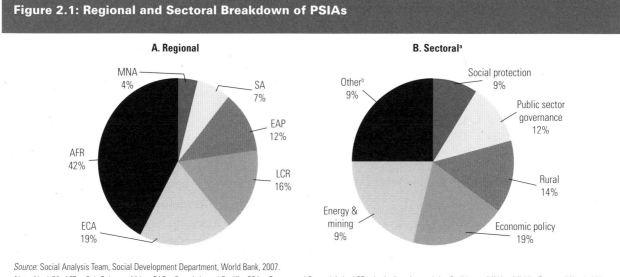

Figure 2.1: Regional and Sectoral Breakdown of PSIAs

A. Regional

MNA 4%
SA 7%
EAP 12%
LCR 16%
AFR 42%
ECA 19%

B. Sectoral[a]

Other[b] 9%
Social protection 9%
Public sector governance 12%
Rural 14%
Economic policy 19%
Energy & mining 9%

Source: Social Analysis Team, Social Development Department, World Bank, 2007.
Note: N =1 56. AFR = Sub-Saharan Africa; EAP = East Asia and Pacific; ECA = Europe and Central Asia; LCR = Latin America and the Caribbean; MNA = Middle East and North Africa; SA = South Asia.
a. Sector is classified by network/sector board.
b. Other includes water; health, nutrition, and population; education; multisectoral; and so forth.

PSIA's objectives; these differences indicate a lack of clarity of purpose.

PSIA Practice versus Initial Concept

PSIAs can incorporate any or all of the following characteristics noted in the Bank's PSIA User's Guide (World Bank 2003h) and the PSIA Good Practice Note (World Bank 2004f):

- Assessing the impact of a well-specified reform
- Using a combination of quantitative and qualitative methods
- Identifying stakeholders—beneficiaries or those adversely affected by the reform as well as proponents and opponents
- Identifying the implementing institutions
- Analyzing risks to reform implementation
- Setting up systems for monitoring and evaluation
- Ensuring stakeholder participation
- Undertaking dissemination.

Although not every PSIA is expected to reflect all dimensions of good practice, many of the characteristics discussed in this chapter are desirable in most country contexts. The discussion in this chapter is based on a portfolio review of the statistically representative sample of 58 PSIAs, although a few references are also made to the country case reviews.

About two-thirds of the sampled PSIAs assessed the impact of a well-specified reform.[1] Although PSIAs originated with concern about the impact of reform programs, about one-third of the sampled PSIAs did not examine well-specified reforms; they were more general sector or macroeconomic analyses.[2] As the PSIA User's Guide notes (World Bank 2003h), robust distributional analysis will generally be easier for well-specified reforms. Preparing PSIAs further upstream in the process of developing reforms may allow for the consideration of a broader range of policy options, but unless the PSIA is linked to well-specified reforms, it may be impossible to undertake meaningful distributional analysis.[3]

An example of a PSIA undertaken to analyze a well-specified reform is the 2007 Montenegro electricity price PSIA (World Bank 2007e). The PSIA took place while the government was preparing an electricity tariff reform that would significantly increase electricity tariffs for residential consumers. Through an ex ante investigation of the welfare impact of this price increase on households in Montenegro, the PSIA showed that the anticipated price increase would result in a significant increase in households' energy expenditures; it included a simulation of alternative policy measures.

In comparison, contrary to the original intent of PSIAs, a 2002 paper on the impact of the Indonesian financial crisis (World Bank 2002) was categorized as a PSIA but did not examine any reform or offer any policy recommendations. It was more of a general look at the poverty effects of the financial crisis.

About half of the sampled PSIAs used a combination of quantitative and qualitative techniques.[4] Slightly fewer than half of the PSIAs relied on purely quantitative economic analyses (appendix table F.2) such as descriptive statistics or regression analysis of household survey data, benefit incidence analysis, social accounting matrices, growth-incidence curves, microsimulation, or computable general equilibrium models. Qualitative methods included stakeholder analysis, institutional analysis, social impact assessment, focus groups, and targeted interviews. In Guyana, for example, the sugar sector PSIA (World Bank 2006f) used semistructured stakeholder interviews and pair-ranking methods to explain and expand on the quantitative findings from the household survey.

Stakeholder identification in PSIAs has been variable. About one-third of the PSIAs explicitly identified beneficiaries or those adversely affected, and about half—although not explicitly identifying beneficiaries or those adversely affected—did include disaggregated data or results (appendix table F.3a). Furthermore, about half identified proponents or opponents of the reform (appendix table F.3b).

The Mauritania mining sector PSIA (World Bank 2006l) is an example of a PSIA that identified both beneficiaries and those adversely affected

and opponents and proponents of a reform. It spelled out who stood to benefit as well as who would likely lose from the proposed reform and detailed which stakeholders would likely oppose the reform. It went on to suggest ways to lessen the negative impact on those who might be adversely affected and to gain the acceptance of potential opponents.

About half of the sampled PSIAs analyzed data specific to women or discussed effects on them. Among the PSIAs covered by the country case reviews, for example, the Cambodia social concessions of land reform PSIA (World Bank 2004a), the Mozambique education PSIA (World Bank 2005h), and the Zambia land, fertilizer, and infrastructure PSIA (World Bank 2005l) discussed gender-specific issues. As with other stakeholder groups, the importance of specifically analyzing impacts on women in the PSIA will depend on the type of policy reform in question.

About half of the sampled PSIAs used a combination of quantitative and qualitative techniques.

About 60 percent of the sampled PSIAs identified the institutions responsible for implementing the reform (appendix table F.4).[5] Institutions are the primary agents through which reforms are implemented. In many cases, identifying which institutions will be responsible for implementation and assessing their capacity is crucial for ensuring the effectiveness of the reform and understanding what the distributional impacts might be. The Sierra Leone mining sector reform PSIA (World Bank 2007f) contained such analysis, including details about which government institution was responsible for overseeing the implementation of specific policies. It described the capacity constraints of key government institutions, coordination problems between relevant ministries, and the role of local leaders, including chiefs, in the mining sector.

About 60 percent of the PSIAs identified the institutions responsible for implementing reform.

About two-thirds of the sampled PSIAs analyzed the risks of implementing the reform program. The risks included institutional capacity risks, political economy risks, market risks, weather risks, and so forth. For instance, the Egypt social policy reform PSIA

Stakeholder participation and the extent and nature of dissemination varied. (World Bank 2005c) noted that the implementation of its recommended reforms would encounter political risks. It also incorporated a sensitivity analysis that involved simulations of different energy price and subsidy scenarios.

About three-quarters of the sampled PSIAs did not suggest key indicators or a data collection method for monitoring and evaluating the reform, policy, or sector in question. Appendix table F.6 shows that monitoring and evaluation has been a weak aspect of PSIAs. For example, although the 2004 Bolivia PSIA (World Bank 2004o) on the impact of hydrocarbon price increases thoroughly addressed various scenarios for increased fuel prices, it did not formulate a system by which the Bank or the Bolivian government could follow the effects of a price increase. This would have been useful not only to validate the accuracy of the predicted effects, but also to provide feedback to tailor the subsidy mechanism or other reform feature aimed at protecting the poor.

There was wide variability in stakeholder participation.[6] The PSIA User's Guide (World Bank 2003h) points out that the process of policy debate, including among stakeholders, can be just as important as the analysis. The wider development literature also points to the importance of broad ownership and of stakeholder participation and consultation to achieve that ownership. More than half of the sampled PSIAs included some sort of stakeholder participation, but for about two-fifths of the PSIAs no consultations were mentioned (appendix table F.7).

The exact degree and nature of participation needed in a specific case will depend, among other things, on the type of policy under consideration, counterpart capacity, political sensitivity of the policy, and operational objectives. But some stakeholder consultation will be necessary in all cases where stakeholder buy-in is critical to the success of the reforms.

The extent and nature of dissemination of PSIAs have varied. Dissemination of PSIAs has been more frequent at the back end (draft or final report stages) than at the front end (concept paper or background work stages) and has been most common among government officials (appendix tables F.8 and F.9). Where English is not widely spoken, only 60 percent of the sampled PSIAs were translated into a local language (appendix table F.10). Almost 60 percent of the sampled PSIAs have been made available on the Internet (appendix table F.11).

Dissemination can help sell the analysis and improve the uptake of recommendations for PSIAs intending to inform country policies. However, wide public dissemination may not always be possible. For example, if a government asks for the Bank's advice on a highly sensitive reform decision on a confidential basis, dissemination must be at the discretion of that government. Nevertheless, it is helpful to disseminate where possible.

This chapter has revealed that PSIAs have widely varying characteristics and that practice has often departed from the initial concept. Some variation in the characteristics of PSIAs is to be expected, given the varying country contexts in which they are undertaken. However, many of the characteristics discussed in this chapter are desirable in most country contexts.

The characteristic that PSIAs have most frequently adopted has been analysis of risks. The most neglected dimensions have been explicitly stating operational objectives, clearly identifying beneficiaries and those adversely affected by the reform, and setting up monitoring and evaluation systems. Overall, the sampled PSIAs had some weaknesses with regard to factors that are important for country ownership and impact on policy making.

Chapter 3

Evaluation Highlights

- This evaluation suggests that on average the PSIAs evaluated had a moderate effect on country policies, with some outstanding examples, and a negligible contribution to country analytic capacity, with a few positive examples.
- A number of factors need to be met if PSIAs are to be effective at the country level: relevance of PSIA topic to country priorities, timeliness, and treatment of the politics of reform. Engaging the appropriate stakeholders can contribute positively toward these factors.
- There is an inherent tension in exerting a timely effect on a country's policy process while also building its analytic capacity.
- Where the impetus for addressing poverty and social impacts comes from external groups and not client governments, client government demand for capacity building cannot be taken for granted.

Indian woman standing in doorway. Photo by Curt Carnemark, courtesy of the World Bank Photo Library.

PSIA Effect at the Country Level

This chapter assesses the in-country effect of PSIAs on two aspects: country policies (including policy debate) and country capacity for policy analysis. The chapter draws on the country case reviews of 12 PSIAs in 8 countries, semistructured stakeholder interviews for an additional 11 PSIAs in 10 countries, the portfolio review, and Independent Evaluation Group (IEG) and non-IEG literature.

Tracing links between PSIA analyses and country decisions is often difficult, especially if the PSIA is only one of many sources of possible influence. PSIA effects may also be diffuse and may occur in the future, as a report may have no discernable impact on immediate action yet may affect ideas and debate that shape future policy choices. This evaluation focuses only on near-term effects of PSIAs.

It is also important to note that strong or weak performance with regard to one operational objective is not the same as high or low effectiveness of a PSIA overall. A PSIA may be effective for one goal and ineffective for others. Indeed, certain goals may be inconsistent with others.

Effect on Country Policies

Extent

The PSIAs reviewed in this evaluation suggest a moderate effect on country policies, on average, although there are some outstanding examples of substantial effect. The criteria used to assess the effect of PSIAs on country policies are presented in box 3.1. Appendix D provides details of these effects for the 12 PSIAs included in the country case reviews. The 11 additional PSIAs that IEG assessed through 48 semistructured stakeholder interviews (with 47 stakeholders, including one stakeholder who was interviewed on two PSIAs), which did not include independent field verification, yielded somewhat more positive but still moderate results on average (see appendix E). The portfolio review discussed in chapter 2 showed that the sampled PSIAs had some weaknesses with regard to factors that are important for country ownership and effect on policy making. Identification of relevant stakeholders—that is, beneficiaries and those adversely affected by the reform, as well as stakeholder participation—has been variable. These findings also point toward a moderate rating for PSIA effect on country policies on average.

Cambodia offers a good example of positive PSIA impact. Land reform was a key poverty

---

Box 3.1: Criteria to Assess PSIA Effect on Country Policies

Substantial: The PSIA contributed to the design and/or adoption of government action (such as legislation, regulation, or decree) or to launching or altering a policy (or set of policies) or program (for example, the government/parliament issues a decree or passes law addressing major points of PSIA).

Moderate: The PSIA contributed to policy deliberation/debate but without affecting follow-on policy action; there was follow-on policy action, but it was not clearly attributable to the PSIA; and/or the PSIA affected only a peripheral aspect of the PSIA's

policy or program recommendations (for example, the government implements some efficiency improvements proposed in the PSIA but not the overall findings on the need for broad institutional reform).

Negligible: The PSIA had little or no discernable impact on policy debate or actions undertaken by the government (for example, the PSIA was devoid of policy recommendations and did not feed into a policy debate or decision in the country).

Source: World Bank.

---

reduction strategy paper objective, and results from the PSIA on social land concessions provided critical analytical inputs that helped implement this national priority (World Bank 2004a). The state land management subdecree of 2007, which addressed many of the deficiencies of the previous land laws, was fostered by the knowledge and consensus gained during the PSIA. This subdecree provided the necessary legal framework to identify and manage land concessions at the local level. The PSIA identified clear problems with the existing legal framework and suggested movement toward resolution of these problems. The PSIA also helped build support within the government for a smallholder-based agricultural development scheme.

Before 2003, many in government felt that efficiency in agriculture and investments in the sector would best be stimulated by supporting large-scale agricultural development. The PSIA, by focusing on potential impacts of smallholder development and identifying how smallholder agriculture could succeed, helped change this perception and built support for the government's subsequent smallholder-based project, Land Allocation for Social and Economic Development. Factors explaining this effect are discussed in box 3.2.

The Mozambique education PSIA (World Bank 2005h) also had a substantial effect on country

policies. Qualitative interviews conducted as part of the PSIA revealed to government officials the numerous additional expenses parents pay when they send their children to school and the variation across districts. In addition, as a result of the PSIA research, the government gained a greater understanding of the role of gender in access to education as well as the particular challenges that orphans face regarding education. The extensive information on supply and demand factors that influence access to education, as discussed in the PSIA, shaped government thinking on the sector. Many of the concerns highlighted in the PSIA regarding access to education by the most vulnerable members of society are echoed in the government's second strategic plan of education.

Explanatory factors for weak effect

There were a number of reasons PSIAs had a moderate or negligible effect on country policies. They suffered, for example, from bad timing, poor choice of topic, or lack of attention to the politics of reform.

The following factors emerge as explanations for the extent or lack of PSIA effect on country policies:

- Operational focus of the PSIA
- Match between PSIA topic and country priorities

Box 3.2: Factors in the Success of the Cambodia Land Reform PSIA

The central importance of land reform to the government of Cambodia contributed to the relevance of the PSIA and enabled its direct insertion into the national policy dialogue. The ex ante nature of the analysis and its timing relative to key policy decisions also helped increase its relevance.

The land reform PSIA was frank about institutional weaknesses, particularly at the level of technical support units for local land use allocation committees. This information helped frame a clear path for successful implementation of the program. The PSIA also identified key weaknesses in enabling legislation and a lack of clear guidance in the legal framework for local decision makers. These institutions were strengthened in subsequent years partly as a result of the high profile the PSIA afforded these institutional weaknesses.

The focus on institutions necessary for reform success helped stimulate further policy changes: prior to 2003, the government knew that additional legislation was needed (such as the 2007 subdecree), and the PSIA provided concrete guidance about elements of the subdecree. The analysis also produced important information about complementary services and support needed to ensure that smallholder households would benefit after they received concession land. The government used this informa-tion in subsequent dialogue with donors about projects needed to support the social land concession program. The availability of complementary services, such as technical assistance, input supplies, marketing services, and so forth, represents an essential component of reform sustainability.

The inclusiveness of the process (with government, NGOs, and civil society participating) and the transparent, qualitative nature of the analysis won the confidence of the government. Stakeholder participation was broad and active. The primary government partner—the Ministry of Land Management, Urban Planning, and Construction—was directly responsible for planning and implementing land policies. Its participation built a strong institutional base of support within the government. The same ministry was also engaged in the analysis of available land.

From this experience it was able to understand the multiple problems associated with identifying and quantifying such land. First-hand experience was invaluable. The ministry was engaged from the very start of the PSIA and continued its involvement through the end (and beyond). The analysis did not rely on abstract models or methods, and the simplicity of the analysis stimulated acceptance.

Sources: Country case review (appendix D), World Bank (2004a).

- Government ownership
- Engagement with parts of the government that have policy jurisdiction over the area covered by the PSIA
- Engagement with appropriate nongovernmental stakeholders
- Consistency of PSIA timing with regard to the country's decision-making process
- Political economy issues being addressed
- Dissemination beyond the distribution of reports.

Informing a policy process is not easy and requires that several of these factors come together—where most of the factors were addressed, the PSIAs had a greater effect. The examples cited below under each factor provide guidance pertaining to that particular factor. The explanatory factors that emerge from this evaluation are similar to those identified in other analyses of the impact of ESW, notably IEG's recent evaluation of the effectiveness of ESW and technical assistance (IEG 2008).

Operational focus of the PSIA. PSIAs that lacked an operational focus failed to adequately inform country policies, regardless of the soundness of their economic analyses. For example, the Mali cotton PSIA work provided descriptive information and poverty estimates based on simulations and models that could not easily be transformed into policy advice. The economic analysis in the PSIA was of high quality and provided useful data on the cotton sector. However, because it did not identify what specific policies the analysis would inform or explicitly specify concrete policy actions, and because it was not widely

Achieving policy influence is not easy—many factors need to come together for a substantial effect on country policies, although not all factors apply equally and unambiguously in all cases.

disseminated, its ability to inform country policies remained low.

In semistructured stakeholder interviews, interviewees noted that although a PSIA in Egypt (World Bank 2005c) helped the Ministry of Social Solidarity build an "environment for change," it could have been more influential had it elaborated on how the safety net could actually be designed and developed. In Nepal, stakeholders pointed out that it is better to conduct PSIAs along with ongoing lending and analytical products, particularly development policy lending, which are the focus of the policy makers' attention.

Match between PSIA topic and country priorities. Close alignment with country priorities was a feature of the more influential PSIAs. Notably, in Cambodia the government had demonstrated its concern with the topic of the land reform by beginning to clarify the 2001 Land Law, issuing its first subdecree on the subject in March 2003. The PSIA began in September of the same year, feeding directly into the government's interest and ongoing policy discussions with other stakeholders around the role of land and its importance to agricultural growth and development. The Cambodia PSIA (World Bank 2004a) also exhibited a number of success factors beyond the relevance of its topic (box 3.2). In Mongolia, the stakeholders interviewed through the semistructured interviews believed that the choice of the PSIA topic—the cashmere sector— was appropriate given Mongolia's dependence on cashmere and the vulnerability of cashmere herders (World Bank 2003c). In contrast, the Ghana Energy PSIA addressed issues of lifeline tariff and consumption inefficiencies that had support from some parts of government, but there was no clear consensus within government about the importance of these issues (World Bank 2004e).

Government ownership. Sufficient support for the PSIA among government officials in relevant agencies and in decision-making positions is essential from early on; otherwise, the chances of having an impact are slight,

regardless of the technical quality of the analysis. The cases reviewed for this evaluation revealed several PSIAs with insufficient government buy-in.

In Nicaragua, the fiscal PSIA (World Bank 2003a) was conducted when the country was about to become eligible for debt relief under the enhanced Heavily Indebted Poor Countries Initiative. In this context, the government was likely to go along with suggestions from the Bank. Indeed, several PSIAs were carried out in Nicaragua at the prompting of IMF and World Bank staff, with the acquiescence—but not the full buy-in—of the government of Nicaragua. Similarly, the water PSIA (World Bank 2005j) in that country was carried out under considerable prodding from the Bank, the Inter-American Development Bank, and others, and a reform was launched to privatize water and sanitation services, but without full government ownership. In both these cases, the effect of the PSIAs on country policies was negligible.

In semistructured stakeholder interviews conducted for this evaluation, interviewees said that the 2006 social protection PSIA work in Indonesia (World Bank 2006k) was successful because the Bank was dealing with a new government that was committed to poverty reduction and job creation. The main lesson to be learned from the semistructured interviews in Sri Lanka was that there has to be a sense of ownership and urgency from the counterpart, without which the Bank should not push PSIA. If the Bank does so, the effort may enhance the Bank's knowledge base but not the government's.

A stakeholder from Sri Lanka suggested including a milestone in the PSIA process that would require that a high-level government panel be established before the concept note stage to ensure ownership of the process. Another stakeholder noted that the way the Bank sometimes conducts PSIAs—hiring a private sector agency or NGO to do the consultations and analytical work—implies that the agency works more closely with the Bank than with the government.

A PSIA can be designed to have immediate impact if government buy-in exists. In circumstances with little initial buy-in, there could still be a case for conducting PSIA if the Bank ascertains there is a high probability that there may be a future opening, but in this case up-front clarity about the time horizon and strategy for impact will be necessary, with the scope and timing of the PSIA designed to maximize the prospects for winning the attention of decision makers over time. In situations that the Bank anticipates a policy issue that is not yet high on the government's agenda, it can try to call attention to that issue through policy dialogue and a PSIA. It can also consider separate initiatives to build awareness and sensitivity to distributive issues or options for institutional reform, such as study tours or training for key officials or politicians. Such anticipatory effort may or may not succeed, but in any case, it should focus on informing country stakeholders, not imposing views on country stakeholders.

Engagement with parts of the government that have policy jurisdiction over the area covered by the PSIA. To have governments "own" the PSIA findings and implement them requires that the Bank engage with parts of the government that have policy and implementation jurisdiction over the area covered by the PSIA. The PSIA analyzing Mozambique's labor policies (Ministry of Planning and Development, Mozambique, and World Bank 2006) was conducted with the Ministry of Planning and Development, but the PSIA team had little contact with the Ministry of Labor. This prevented the PSIA from thoroughly evaluating alternatives to the reform and obtaining full support for them.

In Zambia, the Ministry of Agriculture and Cooperatives was not included in the research, writing, or discussion of the PSIA (World Bank 2005l), even though the issues were under its jurisdiction (which some staff attributed to the PSIA being carried out in association with the Country Economic Memorandum, which had a different country counterpart). The PSIA team in Bangladesh conducted stakeholder consultations with 11 different groups who would be affected by port reform, including the Chittagong Port Authority, but neglected to substantively consult relevant parts of the government on the design, analysis, or drafting of the study, even though they were major stakeholders in the port. The PSIA acknowledged this: "We appreciate there are many gaps in the text below and the annexes, not least because the opinions of the main decision makers—the Ministry of Shipping, National Revenue Board and Ministry of Finance—were not canvassed for their opinions" (World Bank 2005e, p. 8).

Timing of the PSIA should capitalize on a policy opening, although there may sometimes be a role for anticipatory analytical work.

Engagement with the appropriate nongovernmental stakeholders. Identifying beneficiaries and those adversely affected, as well as proponents and opponents of policy reform, and putting measures in place to address them, ideally incorporating their input, can increase the chances of the PSIA informing country policies. The Zambia land, fertilizer, and rural infrastructure PSIA (World Bank 2005l) exemplifies good practice in nongovernmental stakeholder engagement. The PSIA team commissioned participatory poverty research in 10 communities and engaged government officials, business leaders, farmers' unions, NGOs, and other donors throughout the study. This enriched the analysis greatly. The PSIA, drawing on the insights thus gained, uncovered several risks in the proposed land law and recommended against going forward with that law. The government has indeed not moved forward, and though it does not attribute this to the PSIA, another stakeholder does.

The Bank has sometimes engaged that has parts of the government that has no policy jurisdiction over the area covered by the PSIA.

The Republic of Yemen water PSIA also exemplifies good practice with regard to stakeholder involvement (see box 3.3).

In contrast, stakeholders interviewed through semistructured interviews believed that in Armenia the low levels of consultations with NGOs led to a lack of focus on the need to accompany privatization with building awareness of consumers, which they saw as being necessary in a market economy. Stakeholders in Benin were

Box 3.3: Republic of Yemen Water PSIA: Participation by Government, Other Local Stakeholders, the World Bank, and Other Donors

The Republic of Yemen water PSIA, carried out jointly by the Bank, Germany, and the Netherlands, took advantage of GTZ's activity in the sector and involved its resident advisor in the Yemeni government in the effort. Strong partnership among these donors, the government, and other stakeholders—such as consultative councils, water associations, water corporations, civil society organizations, and donors—ensured that the findings of the PSIA would feed into the update of the national water sector strategy.

This strong partnership was achieved through broad engagement of stakeholders that started at the design stage.

Early in the process, donors and stakeholders worked together to determine the methodology and the relevant subsectors. They then commented on a preliminary draft and were again involved in a third stage when their feedback was sought on how to use the findings to update the national water sector strategy and how to use the findings in the design of the subsequent multidonor sector-wide approach, which was funded by the same donors that supported the PSIA, with the addition of DFID.

Sources: World Bank (2007j) and IEG interviews with Bank staff.

adamant that unless the Bank worked with civil society, such as the private sector, farmers' associations and organizations, and the media, there would not be a change in the corruption and patronage that, in their opinion, allowed cartels to operate. According to them, there needed to be more faith in the private sector and in farmers' organizations, as they could force government and the public administration to actually implement policy changes.

Broad public consultation and participation may not always be appropriate if the goal is to affect government decisions. The Indonesia fuel price PSIA of 2005 (World Bank 2005g) addressed a situation where fuel subsidies had become a severe drain on the budget and had a regressive impact. Yet earlier attempts to raise fuel prices had provoked riots. The PSIA analyzed various pricing options and their implications for the budget and for poor households and proposed using savings from removing the fuel subsidy to finance targeted benefits in education, health, and village infrastructure. The analysis was conducted jointly with Indonesian academics and think tanks but was not broadly discussed in public because of the political sensitivity of the issue, although a public information campaign was subsequently mounted by the government.

The PSIA directly and strongly affected both fuel price policy and use of the savings to fund compensatory programs for the poor (World Bank 2005g; IEG 2009, box 4.1).

PSIA timing in regard to the country's decision-making process. A PSIA that is timed to coincide with the decision-making process in a country is likely to be influential. The Cambodia social concessions of land reform PSIA (World Bank 2004a) came at an opportune time for three reasons: Existing institutional arrangements for transferring land to the poor were proving inadequate; a growing consensus was emerging in support of social land concessions; and the government was interested in investigating the impacts of such a program. The semistructured interviews conducted for this evaluation also showed the importance of getting the timing right.

The fuel price increases in Nepal coincided with the country's dialogue about that reform. The PSIA's results were presented to policy makers and informed their decision to raise petroleum prices (World Bank 2005i). In Armenia, semistructured interviews showed that stakeholders believed the PSIA (World Bank 2001d) was done at a time when the government was embarking on privatizing utilities in the country and was keen to have information on its options.

In contrast, the Mozambique labor PSIA (Ministry of Planning and Development, Mozambique, and World Bank 2006) was carried out too late to inform proposed labor law reforms that had already been widely discussed and submitted to Parliament. In Mongolia, interviewees in the semistructured interviews pointed out that although the cashmere PSIA was relevant at the time of its initiation, delays in completion resulted in the loss of interest among various stakeholders (World Bank 2003c). By the time the PSIA was completed, relevant donor programs that the PSIA could have informed were almost complete.

Stakeholders interviewed through semistructured interviews in Benin suggested that the PSIA (World Bank 2004b) was introduced as a retrospective justification for the Bank's planned cotton sector reform project and could have been introduced earlier. In Sri Lanka, where the PSIA (World Bank 2005k) was conceived after a Learning and Innovation Loan on land titling was received with hostility by civil society, stakeholders noted that the PSIA should have been done before the Bank advocated land reform, not after.

Addressing political economy issues. The more influential PSIAs effectively incorporate political economy considerations and take into account the political motivations that inform governments' policy choices. An understanding of the political economy can reveal why seemingly irrational or inefficient policies persist and can help a PSIA to suggest ways to reform them. For example, the Republic of Yemen water sector reform PSIA (World Bank 2007j; box 3.3) identifies the stakeholders who have significant effect on the water resources and irrigated agriculture reforms and assesses their possible support or opposition. It analyzes separately the roles of Parliament, sheikhs and other large landowners, irrigating farmers, the Ministry of Water and Environment, the National Water Resources Authority, the Ministry of Agriculture and Irrigation, and donors. The report details who

holds power, how this will affect the implementation of the reforms, and how best to proceed with the reform given these present power relations. The recent joint Overseas Development Institute and World Bank report on PSIAs regards the Republic of Yemen water PSIA as an influential study (ODI and World Bank 2009).

A PSIA timed to coincide with country decision making is likely to be influential.

Dissemination and follow-up beyond the distribution of reports. Inadequate dissemination and follow-up reduced the effect of several of the examined PSIAs. The Ghana energy PSIA (World Bank 2004e) was not disseminated broadly or in a timely manner, which affected public discussion of its findings and its effect on country policies. Neither the fiscal nor the water PSIAs in Nicaragua (World Bank 2003a; World Bank 2005j) were adequately disseminated. The Bank decided not to disseminate the Bangladesh port PSIA widely (World Bank 2005e). This decision prevented staff from sharing the report with external partners, who may have been able to use the findings in their interactions with the government.[1, 2]

Semistructured stakeholder interviews suggested that the lack of dissemination was a major source of frustration for stakeholders in Sri Lanka. The PSIA, which reported that restrictions on land sales should only be partial (World Bank 2005k), contrary to prior Bank views on the topic, had not yet been shared with any of the local researchers who had worked on the PSIA team or with stakeholders who had taken part in consultations for the PSIA.

Incorporation of political economy considerations can also improve effectiveness.

In contrast, in semistructured interviews in Nepal, interviewees expressed the view that the PSIA on fuel prices (World Bank 2005i) was disseminated to the appropriate groups. The Bank discussed it with cabinet-level officials and various stakeholders. One of the key dissemination activities—an event—was spearheaded by an academic working on this topic and funded by the Bank. This event brought together students' groups and distributors on the campus to discuss why Nepal needed an automated pricing mechanism.

A government stakeholder appreciated the distribution of summary reports at meetings. The local newspaper also reported on the PSIA.

The country case reviews undertaken for this evaluation strongly suggest that dissemination should not be an afterthought. Effective dissemination generally requires more than one event, and not just after the report is printed.

As emphasized in the IEG evaluation of ESW and technical assistance (IEG 2008), follow-up is also important for policy impact and can take the form of lending, technical assistance, further analytical work, or policy dialogue. For policy impact, the follow-up would need to be with policy makers and groups that influence policy makers, including parliamentarians, leaders of opposition parties, trade unions, business associations, heads of cooperatives, and civil society organizations.

In semistructured stakeholder interviews, interviewees noted that the PSIA in Egypt was the first step and that the government would have preferred a prior agreement in which further stages of assistance were spelled out beforehand. In Mongolia, stakeholders felt that it was important for the Bank to have a project or technical assistance to follow a PSIA. In Nepal, Bank staff felt that no matter how many PSIAs the Bank did, they needed to bring in money or the Bank would always be a marginal player.

In general, the Bank's dissemination strategy must reflect the policy issues and country-specific sensitivities at hand, but the presumption should be in favor of dissemination and disclosure. Sometimes, of course, a government can ask for the Bank's advice on a highly sensitive reform decision on a confidential basis. In such cases, the extent of dissemination must be at the discretion of that government. However, the 2008 PSIA Good Practice Note points out that even in such cases the task team should summarize the key messages from the distributional analysis and make them available to the public (World Bank 2008b).

To conclude, it must be noted that not all factors apply equally and unambiguously in all cases.

In some circumstances, certain factors and approaches may be in tension with others. For instance, a thorough PSIA exploration of political economy issues may sometimes conflict with country ownership of findings. Where high-level officials have financial interests in particular policies that the PSIA suggests should be reformed, the government may not welcome frank discussion of this issue.

Somewhat similarly, the need for buy-in by appropriate operational agencies may conflict to some degree with a candid analysis of institutional capacity to implement a policy or program. Variation in the scope of desirable participation in initiation, discussion, and dissemination has already been noted and is supported by IEG's ESW evaluation (IEG 2008). The 2008 revisions in the Good Practice Note that offers guidance for PSIAs (World Bank 2008b) emphasize the need for flexibility in determining approaches suitable for country circumstances. However, initial lack of consideration of these tensions probably contributed to uncertainty within the Bank regarding the PSIA concept and to skepticism regarding its value.

Contribution to Country Capacity for Policy Analysis

The Bank has expected PSIAs to have a major role in building local capacity. As early as 2003, the PSIA User's Guide noted—

> Building national capacity is key to improving analytical rigor over time, in tandem with strengthened country ownership. Many low-income countries have limited capacity and experience in areas of critical importance to PSIAs. These areas include data collection systems, monitoring and evaluation systems, the capacity to conduct analysis and to translate data and analysis into policy, and the institutional structures and mechanisms for debate on such policy issues in the public domain. Building national capacity in these areas must be a fundamental cross-cutting aspect of PSIA. Development partners, including the Bank, have an

important role in strengthening national capacity and in filling analytical gaps. PSIA approaches that foster "learning by doing" should undergird development partners' assistance to countries (World Bank 2003h).

This attention to local capacity building was reinforced in the 2004 PSIA Good Practice Note, which stated, "PSIA is primarily the responsibility of borrower governments. But the Bank and other development partners have a major role in building local capacity for PSIA," and went on to identify three levels of capacity building for PSIAs (World Bank 2004f, paras. 4, 11).

Extent

The PSIAs reviewed in this evaluation suggest a negligible contribution to country analytic capacity, on average, although there are a few examples of substantial contribution. The criteria used to assess the effect of PSIAs on country analytic capacity are presented in box 3.4. Appendix D provides details of these effects for the 12 PSIAs included in the country case reviews. The 11 additional PSIAs assessed by IEG through 48 semistructured stakeholder interviews, which did not include independent field verification, yielded somewhat more positive results—moderate, on average—although this result is based only on 25 observations (23 of the 48 stakeholder interviews yielded no assessment of this dimension; see appendix

E).[3] The recent joint ODI and World Bank report on PSIAs found that the "record on capacity strengthening is weak" (ODI and World Bank 2009).

Building capacity has not been a strong suit of PSIAs.

The one instance among the country case reviews where the PSIA made a substantial contribution to country capacity was the Ghana energy PSIA (World Bank 2004e). In Ghana, considerable training inputs were provided by external consultants and the Bank team, and new methods were introduced in the Kumasi Institute of Technology and Environment, which was contracted as the local consultant for the PSIA. Its staff benefited from the training in qualitative research, which was further enhanced through continuous discussions and reviews.

The Electricity Company of Ghana also benefited in terms of capacity building from the energy PSIA. The company attached a member of its staff to the consultant teams that undertook the survey on which much of the PSIA report was based. As a result, the company learned a great deal about their customers, for example, related to billing arrangements in compound houses. Four years later, and despite nonimplementation of the PSIA's recommendations, the company continues to regard the energy PSIA as having helped build capacity.

In semistructured stakeholder interviews in Albania, Bank staff noted that the PSIA (World

---

Box 3.4: Criteria to Assess PSIA Contribution to Country Capacity

Substantial: PSIA contributed to the transfer of skills or methodologies for gathering and analyzing information on distributional impacts to unit(s) within the government or private institutions (for example, ministry staff gain skills to carry out PSIA).

Moderate: PSIA contributed to the transfer of some skills or methodologies, such as gathering data or stakeholder interviews, to unit(s) within the government or private institutions,

but these skills dealt with only a limited part of the analysis (for example, local consultants participated in the PSIA, but only in the gathering of qualitative data and not in measurement or monitoring of impacts).

Negligible: Little or no transfer of skills and/or methodologies was acquired at the institutional level (for example, PSIA is conducted by a foreign consulting firm with little to no input from locals).

Source: World Bank.

Bank 2004k) improved capacity of the local NGO that had never conducted a PSIA before. The Bank conducted several training workshops with the local NGO director and six or seven local sociologists, shared PSIA resource books, and continued the dialogue to share knowledge going forward, but Bank staff noted that more was needed.

PSIAs have used two main mechanisms to build country capacity. Most PSIAs have involved local stakeholders (such as government ministries, local consultants, or local NGOs) on the PSIA team, relying on learning by doing to build capacity (appendix table F.12).[4] The level of involvement of local stakeholders and the degree of resulting capacity building has, however, differed across PSIAs. The other mechanism has been capacity building through formal training. Training workshops on the use of analytical software were held in the context of the Mali cotton sector PSIA work, and training in participatory monitoring was provided in the case of the Zambia land, fertilizer, and roads PSIA (World Bank 2005l). For the most part, these mechanisms have made a limited contribution to capacity building because the number of skills covered and the length of time spent in training have not generally been significant.

Capacity building needs to be recognized as an objective in its own right and not be treated as a by-product.

Furthermore, PSIAs have sometimes been carried out primarily by Bank staff or have simply been contracted out to foreign consultants, as in Mongolia (World Bank 2003c) or Nicaragua (World Bank 2003a), thereby contributing very little to local capacity building.

Explanatory factors

There are tensions between the objectives of informing country policies in real time and building lasting country analytic capacity.

There are two key factors affecting a PSIA's contribution to country analytic capacity:

Having an explicit capacity building objective and a strategy to achieve it. The first feature of good practice capacity building is recognizing capacity building as a goal in its own right where such a goal is justified by the Country Assistance Strategy. Although a PSIA may or may not include a capacity building objective, in cases where such an objective is justified, the PSIA needs to explicitly state it and specify what kinds of capacity it intends to promote and the organizations to be targeted. Capacity building cannot be treated as a by-product.

There will also need to be a strategy to achieve the intended capacity building over the intended time period. Ensuring that there is demand for capacity from governments will have to be an important part of the strategy, especially because the impetus for PSIAs and evidence-based policy making may not come from client governments. Where capacity building is a PSIA goal, at least some team members will need to be selected for their ability to work with and transfer skills to host country personnel. Two important aspects of the capacity building effort include a needs assessment to precede the specific capacity building intervention and outcome monitoring to be concurrent with it.

Allowing sufficient time for capacity to be built. Capacity building of any lasting sort cannot be hurried and usually needs to be on a slower track than a typical PSIA. It also needs to be reinforced over time. Depending on country circumstances, a programmatic approach that enables successive capacity building investments over a longer period may be more effective in building capacity than a one-off effort.

There is often a tension between the objective of making a real-time contribution to a country's decision-making process (for which the window of opportunity can close quickly) and building country analytic capacity (which is typically a slower and longer process). This tension means that a single approach cannot be used to pursue both these objectives. If capacity building is the objective, then the PSIA approach needs to be specifically tailored to it.

Chapter 4

Evaluation Highlights

- The PSIAs reviewed in this evaluation suggest on average a moderate effect on Bank operations, with some outstanding examples. Interviews conducted for this study indicate that there is not a common understanding among Bank staff about what a PSIA is or should be.
- Operational staff have not been sufficiently engaged in PSIAs, which may have reduced the PSIAs' potential relevance to country assistance programs.
- Staff directly involved with PSIAs see a number of corporate benefits, notably the creation of an important body of knowledge through PSIA guidance.
- Quality assurance, monitoring, and evaluation of the overall effectiveness of PSIAs have been weak.

Villagers playing traditional Cambodian music for tourists in Angkor Wat.
Photo by Masaru Goto, courtesy of the World Bank Photo Library.

PSIA Effect within the Bank

This chapter assesses the effect of PSIAs within the Bank at two levels: Bank operations (including strategy and analytical work) and thinking and practice across the Bank. The latter can clarify the reasons for PSIA effect (or lack thereof) on Bank operations, one of the operational objectives of PSIAs. This chapter draws on the 12 PSIAs covered in the country case reviews, semistructured stakeholder interviews for an additional 11 PSIAs, and interviews with 30 senior Bank staff and managers.

Effect on Bank Operations

The PSIAs reviewed in this evaluation suggest a moderate effect on Bank operations, on average, with some outstanding examples of substantial effect. The criteria used to assess the effect of PSIAs on Bank operations are presented in box 4.1. Appendix D provides details of these effects for the 12 PSIAs included in the country case reviews. The 11 additional PSIAs assessed by IEG through 48 semistructured stakeholder interviews, which did not include independent field verification, yielded somewhat less positive but still moderate results on average (appendix E).

Two Malawi PSIAs (World Bank 2003f, 2004h) had a substantial effect on Bank operations by informing the first Poverty Reduction Support Grant to Malawi. Both the tobacco and agriculture market closure PSIAs (World Bank 2003f, 2004h) are cited in the grant as key analytical underpinnings that contributed to identifying "several weaknesses in current marketing and institutional arrange-

ments for tobacco, which hinder the efficiency of the sector and limit the pass-through of international prices to smallholders" (World Bank 2007c). Likewise, in Nicaragua the PSIA on fiscal reform (World Bank 2003a) influenced the Bank's Poverty Reduction Support Credit and is also referred to as an analytical underpinning.

Implementation of the PSIA approach has had considerable limitations.

In addition, the Cambodia social concessions of land reform PSIA (World Bank 2004a) had substantial influence on the design of a major Bank investment project. The PSIA presented information on a range of elements central to the land reform issue that the government was addressing. Before 2003, many in the government felt that efficiency in agricultural investments would best be stimulated by supporting large-scale agricultural development. The economic concession program was one manifestation of this belief. By focusing on potential impacts of smallholder development and identifying how smallholder agriculture could succeed, the

---

Box 4.1: Criteria to Assess PSIA Effect on Bank Operations

Substantial: Major elements of the PSIA are reflected in the content of Bank lending program, country strategy, or analytical work (for example, a Bank lending document specifically refers to the PSIA as informing the design of the project).

Moderate: Some findings, but not the main points or recommendations of a PSIA, are reflected in the Bank lending program, country strategy, or analytical work (for example, as

a result of a PSIA, the Bank gives greater attention to political economy analysis in the subsequent Country Assistance Strategy).

Negligible: There is little or no impact on Bank lending, country strategy, or analytical work (for example, PSIA findings appear in a Country Economic Memorandum, but as add-ons and with the PSIA's main findings buried).

Source: World Bank.

PSIA helped change this perception and built subsequent support for a smallholder-based project, Land Allocation for Social and Economic Development, which received Bank financing. The PSIA also helped improve relations between the Bank and the government, and the trust built during the process contributed to a smoother and more consensual project design.

The Bangladesh port PSIA (World Bank 2005e) had a moderate effect on Bank operations. There was little collaboration internally within the Bank, notably between the social development unit in the Bank's South Asia Region, where the report was housed, and the transport sector responsible for port strategy. Although some Bank staff say that the PSIA findings led them not to intervene in the port sector, others point to the uncertainties regarding political buy-in as the reason for the lack of follow-up to the PSIA. There was, however, a positive unintended effect from this PSIA: it likely encouraged greater acceptance of political economy analysis in the Bank in general and more political economy analysis of reforms in the preparation of a subsequent Country Assistance Strategy in particular.

In Zambia, apart from the section on rural infrastructure, the substance of the 2005 land, fertilizer, and rural roads PSIA (World Bank 2005l) had a negligible impact on Bank operations. One of the likely reasons was internal policy differences within the Bank, specifically, the

lack of consensus between the PSIA and the Country Economic Memorandum with respect to the emphases they placed on the growth of the private sector in agriculture, the impact of land titling on the poor and vulnerable, the benefits and drawbacks of fertilizer subsidies, and the weight they placed on market solutions for farmers in remote areas. Another reason for the negligible impact may have been the lack of sufficient participation by in-country Bank staff in the PSIA and their resulting lack of ownership of its findings.

Effect on Thinking and Practice across the Bank

Extent

This evaluation has also sought to gauge the effect of the PSIA experience on thinking and practice regarding poverty and social impact analysis across the Bank, based on interviews with 30 senior Bank staff and managers (such as country directors, advisors, and others). They reveal only modest uptake of the PSIA as a robust practice across the Bank, although staff directly involved with PSIAs identified some benefits that the experience has brought to the Bank (box 4.2).[1]

Most Bank management and staff interviewed felt that the utility of PSIAs is yet to be proven and that the uptake of PSIAs by country directors and operational teams remains dependent on individual inclinations rather

Box 4.2: Corporate Benefits Identified by PSIA Proponents

Although there was not a consensus among Bank staff interviewed about the extent of PSIA effects on thinking and practice across the Bank, Bank staff and donors directly involved with PSIAs cited a variety of corporate benefits since fiscal 2002:

- **Innovative analytic framework.** PSIAs have sought to provide an innovative analytical framework that aims to bring economic and noneconomic analysis and quantitative and qualitative evidence together. They have emphasized a participatory process in addition to the analytic approach. These innovations are captured in two quotes from Bank and other donor agency staff: "PSIAs have been transformational in bringing a focus on a more holistic view of development beyond a narrow economic view" and "Like poverty reduction strategy papers, the main contribution of PSIAs has been on the process side."

- **Knowledge and tools.** The analytic work published as part of PSIAs provides an important body of knowledge. In addition, guidance and tools in the form of the PSIA User's Guide, sourcebook, and Good Practice Note are seen as useful not only for PSIAs but also for other analytical work. This has led to increased knowledge about the differential impacts of reforms and how they can be addressed. "More people are aware that all reforms have differential impacts and that they should be acted on. The understanding has always been there, but giving it form and providing the tools does affect how people think and what guidance they have available," said one interviewee. Another said, "The initiative, the branding, the creation of a business line propelled more thinking about distributional issues."

- **Improved Bank risk management.** "The Bank is now more forthcoming, explicit, and systematic in recognizing and managing risks from distributional issues."

- **Enhanced Bank credibility.** Some staff see improved Bank credibility as a result of the introduction of PSIAs, especially anchoring poverty and social impact analysis in a Bank Operational Policy (OP 8.60). "This makes an important statement about the Bank and makes for a different view of the Bank [from] the outside."

Sources: IEG interviews with Bank staff and donors directly involved with PSIAs.

---

than on the need to reflect established practice. As expressed by one country office staff member, although poverty and social impact analysis is now reflected in DPLs, "it still needs to be made a normal part of doing business." This limitation is expressed in the following ways.

Differing views on the nature and importance of PSIAs. There is a vast difference between the institutional view of a PSIA as defined on the Bank's PSIA Web site (World Bank 2008e), the PSIA User's Guide (World Bank 2003h), and the PSIA Good Practice Note (World Bank 2008b) and Bank staff understanding of it. Among interviewees, there was little homogeneity of views about what a PSIA is, how important it is, or how to do it. Most operational staff interviewed lacked a common understanding about the objectives and processes of the PSIA approach. PREM staff generally tended to favor a focus on economic analysis, and SDN staff tended to emphasize mixed methods, including social and institutional analysis and a participatory process.

Emphasis on flexibility. Most Bank staff wanted flexibility in assessing the poverty and social consequences of policy reforms. They felt a PSIA with all the "bells and whistles" was not needed in every—or even most—cases. Is there consensus? "Yes, for poverty and social analysis, but no, for one way of doing it bundled together [conducting economic as well as social, institutional, and political analysis, using both quantitative and qualitative methods, focusing on analytical aspects as well as process, and so forth], in all cases," said one respondent. Bank staff interviewed disagreed about the importance of specific aspects of the PSIA approach.

There is lack of a common understanding among Bank staff about what a PSIA is or should be.

Explanatory factors

Seven factors appear to have had significant bearing on the extent of the effect of PSIA on Bank operations and, more broadly, on thinking and practice in Bank analytical work and the design of country strategies. These factors are—

- Understanding of PSIA as only a product
- Buy-in of country directors
- PSIA team composition and financing
- Complexity and ambiguity of PSIA guidance
- Regional quality assurance processes
- Sufficient engagement between the PSIA team and operational staff in headquarters or country offices
- Link to Bank operations or policy decision.

Understanding of PSIA as only a product. If PSIAs are seen as a product and an end in themselves, the focus on informing Bank operations or country policies might be lower than otherwise expected. Some interviewees referred to large research studies that received funding from the Incremental Fund but that were not embedded in the policy-making process of the client country. "PSIAs were always meant to be part of a policy process, but the Bank went off track with massive studies," said one interviewee. For example, a study on the history of land reform in Vietnam, which provides a technically sophisticated and interesting examination of Vietnam's past land reforms (Do and Iyer 2003), was categorized as a PSIA. Large research papers like this have led to the perception of the PSIA as a "Cadillac product" rather than an approach that involves analysis of poverty and social impacts of policy reforms, as originally intended.

Buy-in of country directors. Country director buy-in for PSIAs has been weak. Several country directors interviewed complained that they barely have enough time for the basic analytical blocks such as Country Policy and Institutional Assessments and therefore view PSIAs as a luxury. The result has been scant incorporation of PSIA work into their country programs. Sector directors appear to be more positive about PSIAs, but interviews with network and country staff and country directors suggest that, for the most part, country

Buy-in from country directors has been weak.

directors are not yet convinced of the utility of the approach relative to other things that have to be done to develop an effective country program. Overall, the success of PSIAs in informing country assistance programs has depended on individual inclinations of Bank staff rather than on established practice.

PSIA team composition and financing. A number of interviewees noted that PSIAs conducted by short-term staff and with outside funding have often failed to attract the attention of Bank staff who are responsible for country lending or analytical work. For example, in Zambia, some members of the PSIA team were short-term consultants and therefore not employed long enough to ensure that the findings remained on the Bank and donor agendas. Furthermore, heavy external funding with a minor Bank budget contribution in this case led the PSIA to be perceived as being external and not sufficiently owned by the Bank. In contrast, the Morocco water supply and sanitation PSIA and the 2007 water sector DPL teams overlapped, so the PSIA (World Bank 2006a) directly informed that DPL.

Complexity and ambiguity of PSIA guidance. The Bank has produced a substantial body of guidance on the PSIA approach, and these materials have been refined over time to incorporate lessons learned. However, most Bank staff interviewed have regarded the materials (such as the 2003 PSIA User's Guide, or 2004 PSIA Good Practice Note) as too onerous and demanding: "Bells and whistles about PSIAs are a turn-off." The 2004 PSIA Good Practice Note (World Bank 2004f) was seen as creating unrealistic expectations and a high standard against which PSIAs would be judged.

Tensions and ambiguities inherent in the PSIA guidance may also have contributed to skepticism among Bank staff. These tensions include the inconsistency, in many circumstances, between strong country ownership and frank examination of political and institutional obstacles and capacities affecting proposed policies and the inconsistencies between exerting timely effect on country (and Bank) decisions and building country analytic capacity. In other words, many Bank staff may view PSIA guidance as unrealistic. Revisions in the 2008 PSIA Good Practice Note (World Bank 2008b) address some of these concerns, but are not yet fully known among Bank staff. The tensions between the capacity building objective and other PSIA operational objectives remain to be addressed.

Regional quality assurance processes. According to interviews with Bank managers and staff, the focus of decision meetings on PSIAs has typically been on the technical quality of assessment. Few questions are asked about the intended effect of PSIAs or the strategy for achieving that effect. For PSIAs to attain their operational objectives, Regional management needs to send clear signals—through questions asked—from the concept stage onward, especially related to process and intended effect. In addition, staff performance assessments need to factor in PSIA effect, not just technical quality. A strengthened Regional quality assurance process that asks the right questions about a PSIA's fit with the country assistance program and a PSIA's effectiveness is crucial.

More systematic use of peer reviewing might focus PSIAs better. Appendix table F.13[2] shows that the PSIA Concept Notes (World Bank 2001b) were peer reviewed in 40 percent of the cases in IEG's portfolio review. The draft PSIA was peer reviewed in 53 percent of cases, although there were several cases for which the existence or lack of peer review was difficult to discern from the documentation.

Sufficient engagement between the PSIA team and operational staff both in headquarters and in country offices. One of the most striking findings of this evaluation is the limited success in engaging Bank operational staff—both at headquarters and in country offices—on PSIA content and process and the associated lack of buy-in from operational staff within the Bank.[3] IEG's country case reviews found this an issue in Mozambique and Ghana, among others. Operational staff found that the Mozambique labor PSIA (Ministry of Planning and Development, Mozambique, and World Bank 2006) did not assess the shortcomings of the new law or examine alternatives, that it lacked data and made claims it could not support, and that it did not clearly assess who the beneficiaries or those adversely affected by the proposed reform might be. Moreover, some operational staff disagreed with the findings, affecting their follow-through. In Ghana, there was insufficient ownership of the PSIA among the Bank's Energy Unit staff, most of whom did not consider distributional issues—the focus of the PSIA—among their main priorities.[4]

Link to Bank operations or policy decision. A PSIA that is not conceived in the context of a proposed Bank-supported policy reform, analytical work, or lending program will typically have only a moderate effect on Bank lending, strategy, or advice. The Bank's research and analytical interests may sometimes generate supply-driven or general analyses not directly linked to the Bank's operational work. The Indonesia micro-macro reform PSIA (World Bank 2002) was a retrospective look at the poverty effects of the financial crisis and was not connected to a lending operation. The Bangladesh port PSIA (World Bank 2005e) also was not linked to a specific lending operation but focused on an analysis of the political economy.

Recent Developments

Two developments have occurred during this evaluation—revision of the Bank's Good Practice Note and discussions on the new Multi-Donor Trust Fund for continued funding of PSIAs. In view of the findings of this evaluation, both initiatives will need to go further than they currently do.

2008 PSIA Good Practice Note

The 2008 PSIA Good Practice Note (World Bank 2008b) is an improvement over the 2004 Good Practice

The 2004 Good Practice Note was seen as creating unrealistic expectations and a high standard against which PSIAs would be judged.

The flexibility granted by the 2008 PSIA Good Practice Note in determining approaches suitable for country circumstances is likely to increase PSIA receptivity among Bank staff.

Bank operational staff have not been sufficiently engaged in the content and process of PSIAs at headquarters or in country offices and therefore have not sufficiently bought into PSIAs.

The initial lack of attention to flexibility may have contributed to uncertainty about the PSIA concept and to skepticism regarding its value.

Note (World Bank 2004f) in that it grants considerable flexibility to Regions in determining the balance among economic, social, institutional, and political analyses (and between quantitative and qualitative techniques), as well as between analytics and such process issues as stakeholder participation and disclosure. This flexibility will allow the scope and content of the PSIA to be better tailored to the specific context and may also help avoid the perception of the PSIA as a "Cadillac product."

However, although flexibility can help improve the relevance of the PSIA to a country context, Bank staff need to provide the rationale for specific choices made. This issue is not recognized in the 2008 PSIA Good Practice Note. Providing such a rationale can help ensure that Bank staff from the different networks will not continue to emphasize their respective disciplinary approaches in undertaking PSIAs.

The 2008 Good Practice Note grants flexibility to the Regions for PSIA content and process.

Another shortcoming of the 2008 PSIA Good Practice Note is that it has not yet fostered a common understanding among Bank staff about what a PSIA is. In fact, the main debates among various groups in the Bank in revising the Good Practice Note have centered on what constitutes a PSIA and what should be called something else. There is no consensus yet among Bank staff about what a PSIA is or should be. This lack of consensus has a strong influence against conducting the relevant analysis and its quality assurance.[5]

New Multi-Donor Trust Fund for PSIAs

The Bank and donors are discussing the Multi-Donor Trust Fund for PSIAs. The use of such earmarked funds for PSIAs requires that the Bank give special attention both to the balance between its own budget and trust fund use and to a strategy for continued engagement beyond the end of earmarked funding. The risks associated with earmarked funds are similar to those related to other infant industry approaches—overinvestment and misallocation during the protection period and a return to underinvestment when protection ends.

The Bank needs to clarify its objectives for PSIA and decide how much and which of the PSIA work it will fund from its own budget and for what it will rely on trust funds. Requiring *all* trust fund allocations to be matched by a substantial Bank contribution (especially from the country unit budget) would help ensure Bank ownership of the work that is financed by the trust funds and its grounding in country assistance programs.

Chapter 5

Three generations at a family-owned store in Kabul, Afghanistan. Photo by Michael Foley, courtesy of the World Bank Photo Library.

Lessons and Recommendations

The PSIA approach has correctly emphasized the importance of understanding the institutional and political constraints to development and the need to build domestic ownership of policy reforms in addition to assessing the distributional impact of policy actions. However, implementation of the approach has had considerable limitations. Nevertheless, the PSIA experience so far suggests several lessons, and some notable successes have modeled what PSIAs can accomplish when done right. The lessons and recommendations in this chapter are intended to help improve future implementation of the PSIA approach and realize its potential.

Lessons

Informing country policies and building country capacity

Participation is important, but how much, when, and with whom depends on the specific context.

PSIAs can adopt different degrees of participation and involve varying stakeholder groups that reflect the particular contexts in which they are undertaken. The exact degree and nature of stakeholder participation that is appropriate in a particular case will depend on, among other things, the type of policy under consideration, counterpart capacity, political sensitivity of the policy, and the operational objectives of the PSIA. Some stakeholder consultation will be necessary in all cases where stakeholder buy-in is critical to the success of reform.

Both design and timing of PSIAs need to take account of the political context.

Adoption of evidence-based policy making can mean major shifts in power relationships. Particularly where policy making has not typically been transparent or there are powerful stakeholders in the sector being analyzed, the PSIA will need to take these political economy considerations into account. An understanding of the political economy of policy making in a country can help ensure that the PSIA fits local decision-making processes and is appropriately timed and designed.

There may be trade-offs between methodological sophistication and capacity building.

Depending on the existing level of capacity in a country, building capacity through learning by doing or short training programs may not be an immediate option, especially in PSIAs that adopt overly sophisticated methodologies. If the PSIA uses complex methodologies, the Bank will need to consider significant pre-investments in training before local stakeholders can be effectively involved in a learning-by-doing capacity building effort. For example, in Mali, the Social Accounting Matrix was technically too sophisticated for most participants; more intensive training would have been required for participants to actually use the tool and to fully understand the results.

Where capacity building is a priority, the Bank should consider whether there are more effective alternatives to a one-time PSIA that also has the objective of informing country policies.

Given the tensions between informing the policy process in a timely manner and building capacity, the same approach is unlikely to effectively serve both objectives. Therefore, the PSIA will need to be tailored to pursuing the particular objective in question. In many cases, technical assistance or other programmatic instruments that are designed as a series or as an incremental package of interventions may be a more effective approach to capacity building than a one-time PSIA. The Bank is currently exploring incremental approaches in three pilot countries whereby a number of different products and approaches can be combined in a sequence over time. The joint ODI and World Bank report on PSIAs outlines some design features of an incremental approach (ODI and World Bank 2009).

Informing Bank operations and thinking and practice across the Bank

A clear understanding of the PSIA approach and its value is needed to obtain support for this analytic work and to ensure the necessary allocation of Bank resources for it.

The lack of clarity among Bank staff about what a PSIA is can create problems for quality assurance and monitoring of the quantity, quality, and effectiveness of PSIAs. Ambiguity can also hinder the appropriate allocation of funds for relevant analysis.

It is important to ensure ownership for PSIA work within the relevant Bank operational units.

Early buy-in for PSIA work from the relevant constituencies *within* the Bank is as essential as buy-in from country stakeholders. Otherwise there is little chance of the analysis having an effect on country strategy, lending, or analytical work, almost regardless of the technical quality of the analysis.

PSIA experience shows that staff ownership depends at a minimum on communication about the scope and content of a PSIA between the analytic team and relevant operational staff; ownership is better when there is close consultation with or actual participation by the Bank's country staff in the analysis. Where a PSIA's analysis runs counter to the prevailing views of operational staff, a process of dialogue will be important. Strong leadership from Bank management will be necessary to ensure that findings that run counter to the common assumptions of one sector unit in regard to another are not buried or ignored, and to resolve differences.

Earmarking of resources has pros and cons.

The availability of special earmarked funds can have both positive and negative effects. On the positive side, interviews with Bank staff and managers indicated that earmarked funding for PSIAs was essential to getting the PSIA work going, and early PSIA work contributed to a body of knowledge on poverty and social impact that otherwise would not have materialized.

On the negative side, earmarked funding has sometimes resulted in supply-driven analysis as researchers accessed the earmarked funds for projects that are not necessarily focused on assessing the poverty and social effects of specific policy reforms but that are more general background analyses. Furthermore, the availability of earmarked funds may have postponed consideration by senior management of whether and how to sustain such analysis with resources from the Bank's budget. By using earmarked trust funds, PSIAs are kept outside of mainstream Bank work and could, therefore, be excluded from the work program agreements at the beginning of each year, with possible adverse effects on PSIA relevance to the country program.

There could also be issues of ownership, as noted by one interviewee: "Because there was relatively minor input from [the Bank's] country staff and the funding came from a trust fund instead of the Regional budget, there was a lack of Bank ownership of this PSIA." As the Bank prepares to obtain and execute the Multi-Donor Trust Fund currently under negotiation, it will be important to identify how the possible negative effects of earmarking can be avoided.

Recommendations

This evaluation makes four recommendations to strengthen the Bank's work using the PSIA approach, whether done as a freestanding analysis or embedded in other analytical work.

- **Ensure that staff understand what the PSIA approach is and when to use it. Bank management can do this by providing clear guidance (perhaps through updating of the 2008 PSIA Good Practice Note) and actively disseminating this guidance, particularly on—**
  - Whether and how the PSIA approach differs from other distributional analyses, including whether the inclusion of the word "social" in Poverty and Social Impact Analysis suggests the need to include a different type of analysis
  - Whether or not PSIAs should be linked to specific reforms and identify beneficiaries and those adversely affected by the reform
  - What criteria should be used to determine when the PSIA approach is appropriate for a particular operation in a country program.
- **Clarify the operational objectives of each PSIA with regard to its intended effect,**

and tailor the approach to those objectives, ensuring that the concept note—
  - Contains a clear statement of the operational objectives of the PSIA with respect to the intended effect (not just the topics/issues to be analyzed)
  - Indicates how its approach—in particular, stakeholder engagement, team composition, partner institutions, budget, and time frame—has been tailored to meet the operational objectives and provides the rationale for the choices made
  - Shows how any tensions and trade-offs among the operational objectives will be reconciled
  - Discusses if the intended dissemination audience and strategy are consistent with the stated operational objectives.
- **Improve integration of the PSIA into the Bank's country assistance program by—**
  - Shifting significant decision-making and funding authority to the Regional Vice Presidencies to ensure that the PSIA topics, scope, and approach are consistent with the country assistance program and that PSIAs ask questions that are relevant to policy
  - Requiring that *all* earmarked funding for PSIAs be matched by a substantial contribution from the country unit budget.
- **Strengthen PSIA effectiveness through enhanced quality assurance, including—**
  - Subjecting PSIAs to systematic review by Regional management at concept and completion stages to ensure relevance and fit of the PSIA to the country assistance program as well as consistency of the proposed approach with operational objectives, in addition to ensuring technical quality
  - Ensuring that the Bank establishes a monitoring and self-evaluation system designed to assess whether PSIAs are being undertaken where appropriate and are achieving their stated operational objectives.

Three Indian women. Photo by Curt Carnemark, courtesy of the World Bank Photo Library.

Appendixes

Colombian children. Photo by Curt Carnemark, courtesy of the World Bank Photo Library.

1987: The World Bank's Operational Guidelines required president's reports supporting structural adjustment loans to "pay particular attention to ... an analysis of the short-term impact of the adjustment program on the urban and rural poor, and measures proposed to alleviate negative effects" (World Bank 1987).

1987–92: Jointly executed by the World Bank, the African Development Bank, and the United Nations Development Programme, the Social Dimensions of Adjustment in Africa Program aimed at helping participating African countries integrate poverty and social concerns in the design and implementation of their adjustment programs to mitigate the burden on the poor in the process of structural adjustment. The program's mandate was to strengthen the capacity of African governments to design appropriate programs and projects in this regard. It also aimed at strengthening the analytical capacity of governments to carry out empirical studies to assess the evolution of socioeconomic conditions of population groups over time.

1996: The World Bank, in conjunction with national governments and a worldwide network of almost 1,000 civil society organizations, launched the Structural Adjustment Participatory Review Initiative to assess the economic and social impact of structural adjustment policies on various social groups in the borrowing countries. The goal was to improve understanding about the impact of adjustment policies and how the participation of civil society can enhance economic policy making. The initiative was to be both a review of past experience and a forward-looking exercise designed to identify practical changes in policy making that could lead to significant improvements in people's lives.[1]

2000: A letter from Oxfam International addressed to International Monetary Fund (IMF) Managing Director Kohler and World Bank President Wolfensohn expressed concern that the Fund and Bank had not met the commitments (made by their respective boards some 15 months earlier in the context of developing Poverty Reduction Strategy Papers [PRSPs]) to assess the impact of proposed reforms in Fund/Bank programs before undertaking reforms (ex ante impact assessments).

2001: The Joint (IMF and World Bank) Implementation Committee for PRSPs acknowledged the gaps in the analysis of policy impacts within client countries and asked the Bank to take the technical lead in helping developing countries fill this analytical gap.

2002: Poverty and Social Impact Analyses (PSIAs) were formally launched within the Bank in fiscal 2002 when a PSIA internal concept note was written. The concept note stated PSIA objectives as to continually inform policy dialogue, choice, and implementation, within the overarching objective of promoting sustainable poverty reduction and social inclusion.

2002: The World Bank and the Department for International Development (DFID) initiated PSIA pilots (and completed six each over the next two-year period).

2003: The donor network for PSIA was established by a range of multilateral and bilateral donor agencies, based on the North Sea Manifesto. The network's objective was to support country-led, participatory, and evidence-based policy making for poverty reduction.

2004: The IMF formally set up a PSIA group of five experts within an existing division in its Fiscal Affairs Department.

2004: The World Bank put International Bank for Reconstruction and Development surpluses into a PSIA Incremental Fund of $5.8 million.

2004: The World Bank adopted Operational Policy 8.60 on Development Policy Loans (DPLs) and the accompanying Good Practice Note, "Using Poverty and Social Impact Analysis to Support Development Policy Operations."

2006: Oxfam wrote to President Wolfowitz requesting that multidisciplinary PSIA be conducted in good time and that analyses consider a range of options, use local researchers, be made public, and be monitored. It also requested that while this was happening in some cases, it happen in most cases going forward.

2007: Efforts of the 2003 donor network for PSIAs were integrated with the Task Team on Ex Ante Poverty Impact Assessments of the Organisation for Economic Co-operation and Development's Development Assistance Committee's Network on Poverty Reduction. Task teams have a two-year span, so this team will come to a close soon.

2007: The Development Assistance Committee approved the practical guide to ex ante Poverty Impact Assessment, a "light" version of PSIA that is less demanding in terms of time and financial resources and focuses more on specific projects and programs than on major policy reforms.

2007: Oxfam met with President Zoellick and requested that PSIA be strengthened and used as consensus-building tools to carry out analysis and promote pro-poor policies. According to Oxfam, PSIA could be mechanisms to not only carry out useful diagnostic studies on the social impacts of poverty, but to help develop policy agreements between governments and the Bank, as well as to ensure civil society participation in the formulation of poverty reduction efforts. This could lead to greater policy choices being considered and greater country ownership. Oxfam expressed concerns that (i) the Bank does not do enough PSIAs; (ii) it does not do enough to build country capacity and to foster country ownership; (iii) there is insufficient disclosure of PSIA results by the Bank; and (iv) PSIAs focus too much on mitigating the impacts of a predetermined reform and not enough on analyzing alternative policy options.

2007: The World Bank, DFID, and the German Agency for Technical Cooperation produced "Tools for Institutional, Political, and Social Analysis of Policy Reform: A Sourcebook for Development Practitioners" (World Bank 2007g).

2008: The Bank updated the Good Practice Note "Using Poverty and Social Impact Analysis to Support Development Policy Operations."

2008: A fresh round of dedicated PSIA Trust Funds came under consideration—a new Multi-Donor Trust Fund for PSIAs is being discussed among the Bank, DFID, GTZ, and some other donors to support country-led PSIAs with an emphasis on developing country capacity for policy analysis.

	Country	Reform	Sector classification	Fiscal year of funding
1	Albania	Pensions	Social Protection	2002
2	Albania	Energy tariffs	Energy and Mining	2002
3	Albania	Decentralization and priv. of water	Water Supply and Sanitation	2003–04
4	Albania	Education	Education	2004
5	**Albania**	**Irrigation and drainage**	**Rural Sector**	**2002**
6	Angola	Fuel and utility	Energy and Mining	2004
7	Argentina	Heads of Households Transition Project	Social Protection	2006
8	**Armenia**	**Utility pricing and the poor**	**Energy and Mining**	**2002**
9	Azerbaijan	Education	Education	2005
10	Azerbaijan	State-owned enterprises	Public Sector Governance	2004–05
11	Azerbaijan	Utility pricing	Multisectoral	2004
12	Bangladesh	Social protection	Social Protection	2004
13	**Bangladesh**	**Chittagong Port**	**Transport**	**2004**
14	**Benin**	**Cotton**	**Rural Sector**	**2003**
15	Bolivia	Teacher salaries	Public Sector Governance	2004
16	Bolivia	Public expenditure	Multisectoral	2004
17	Bolivia	Pension	Public Sector Governance	2004
18	**Bolivia**	**Fuel and liquefied petroleum gas prices**	**Energy and Mining**	**2004**
19	Bosnia-Herzegovina	State-owned enterprises	Public Sector Governance	2005
20	Botswana	Livestock	Rural Sector	2005
21	Brazil	Urban reforms	Urban Development	2005
22	Burkina Faso	Growth inequality linkages	Economic Policy	2004
23	Burkina Faso	Cotton sector	Economic Policy	2002
24	Burkina Faso, Benin, Guinea, Mauritania	Poverty Analysis Macroeconomic Simulator modeling	Economic Policy	2005
25	Burundi	Coffee liberalization	Rural Sector	2005
26	Cambodia	Rice tariffs	Economic Policy/Trade	2002
27	Cambodia	School subsidies	Education	2005
28	**Cambodia**	**Social concessions of land**	**Social Development**	**2004**

(continued on next page)

	Country	Reform	Sector classification	Fiscal year of funding
29	Cameroon	Overall public expenditure program	Economic Policy	2003
30	Cameroon	Health, human capital, and prospects for inclusive economic growth for Cameroon	Health, Nutrition and Population	2006
31	Cape Verde	VAT	Economic Policy	2005
32	Cape Verde	Utility tariffs	Multisectoral	2005
33	**Cape Verde**	**Targeting of social programs**	**Social Protection**	**2006**
34	Chad	Cotton	Rural Sector	2003
35	China	Urban Dibao in China: Building on Success	Social Protection	2005
36	Congo, DR	Forestry	Rural Sector	2005
37	Congo, DR	Mining sector	Energy and Mining	2004
38	**Congo, DR**	**Public sector reform for basic service provision**	**Public Sector Governance**	**2004**
39	**Côte d'Ivoire**	**Public expenditure prioritization**	**Economic Policy**	**2004**
40	Côte d'Ivoire	Trade of cocoa and coffee	Economic Policy/Trade	2005
41	Croatia	Enterprise restructuring	Private Sector Development	2006
42	Croatia	Design of social impact assessment methodology (country-systems approach to PSIA)	Multisectoral	2006
43	**Djibouti**	**Energy sector**	**Energy and Mining**	**2004**
44	Dominica	Public sector	Public Sector Governance	2003
45	Ecuador	Safety net restructuring	Social Protection	2005
46	**Egypt**	**Social policy**	**Social Protection**	**2006**
47	**El Salvador**	**CAFTA**	**Economic Policy/Trade**	**2005**
48	Eritrea	Electricity	Energy and Mining	2005
49	Ethiopia	Road construction impact	Transport	2004
50	Ethiopia	Employment Creation Effects of the Addis Ababa Integrated Housing Programme	Urban Development	2006
51	Ethiopia	Public expenditure prioritization	Transport	2004
52	Ethiopia	Distributional aspects of service delivery	Health, Nutrition, and Population	2007
53	**Ethiopia**	**Health care financing study (distributional and health impacts of health sector development plan interventions)**	**Health, Nutrition, and Population**	**2006**
54	**Ethiopia**	**Enhancing human development outcomes through decentralized service delivery**	**Public Sector Governance**	**2006**
55	Ethiopia	Electricity tariffs	Energy and Mining	2006
56	Georgia	Utilities (water, gas, and electricity tariff increases)	Multisectoral	2002
57	**Ghana**	**Energy pricing and subsidies**	**Energy and Mining**	**2004**
58	Guatemala	Fiscal reform	Economic Policy	2005
59	Guatemala	CAFTA	Economic Policy/Trade	2006

	Country	Reform	Sector classification	Fiscal year of funding
60	Guyana	Water sector	Water Supply and Sanitation	2002
61	Guyana	Bauxite	Energy and Mining	2003–04
62	**Guyana**	**Sugar sector Living Standards Measurement Study**	**Rural Sector**	**2004–05**
63	Honduras	Minimum wage policy (proposal was on civil service reform)	Public Sector Governance	2004–05
64	Honduras	CAFTA	Economic Policy	2003–04
65	**Honduras**	**Fiscal analysis/taxes**	**Multisectoral**	**2003/04/05**
66	India	Agricultural marketing reform impact on India's farmers	Rural Sector	2006
67	**Indonesia**	**Macro reforms**	**Economic Policy**	**2003**
68	**Indonesia**	**Local government**	**Economic Policy**	**2005**
69	**Indonesia**	**Social protection**	**Social Protection**	**2004**
70	Indonesia	Fuel subsidy	Energy and Mining	2004
71	**Indonesia**	**Rice tariff**	**Economic Policy/Trade**	**2002**
72	Indonesia	Severance pay	Economic Policy	2007
73	Kenya	Commodities markets	Public Sector Governance	2006
74	Kenya	Improving targeting of public expenditure to the poor	Economic Policy	2006
75	Kenya	Pension	Social Protection	2005
76	Kenya	Health user fees and waivers	Health, Nutrition, and Population	2005
77	Kenya	Maize prices	Rural Sector	2005
78	Kosovo	State-owned enterprises	Public Sector Governance	2005
79	Kyrgyz Republic	Electricity	Energy and Mining	2006
80	Lao PDR	Analysis of the distributional impact of public expenditures, with a focus on ethnic minorities and women	Economic Policy	2006
81	Lao PDR	Public expenditure and revenue management and increase in utility tariffs	Economic Policy	2004
82	Lesotho	Rural electrification	Energy and Mining	2005
83	**Lesotho**	**Electricity sector**	**Energy and Mining**	**2004**
84	**Madagascar**	**Service delivery—Institutional analysis**	**Public Sector Governance**	**2003**
85	Madagascar	Health care and the poor	Health, Nutrition, and Population	2006
86	**Madagascar**	**Agriculture (rice, fertilizer, infra, transaction, extension)**	**Rural Sector**	**2003**
87	Madagascar	Enhancing land tenure security	Rural Sector	2006
88	Madagascar	Welfare impact of higher energy prices in Madagascar	Energy and Mining	2006
89	Malawi	Electricity	Energy and Mining	2005

(*continued on next page*)

	Country	Reform	Sector classification	Fiscal year of funding
90	**Malawi**	**Tobacco marketing**	**Rural Sector**	**2004**
91	Malawi	Agriculture market closures	Rural Sector	2006
92	**Mali**	**Cotton sector**	**Rural Sector**	**2004**
93	Mauritania	Oil and gas impact on the economy	Energy and Mining	2006
94	**Mauritania**	**Mining services**	**Energy and Mining**	**2004**
95	Mauritania	Water	Water Supply and Sanitation	2002
96	**Mauritania**	**Health**	**Health, Nutrition, and Population**	**2002**
97	Mexico	Implementation of water and forestry policies in Mexico	Environment	2006
98	**Moldova**	**Energy sector**	**Energy and Mining**	**2004**
99	Moldova	Energy price changes	Energy and Mining	2006
100	Mongolia	Energy sector	Energy and Mining	2004
101	**Mongolia**	**Cashmere (trade)**	**Economic Policy/Trade**	**2004**
102	Mongolia	School year	Education	2005
103	**Montenegro**	**Water and sanitation**	**Water Supply and Sanitation**	**2005**
104	**Montenegro**	**Poverty and environmental impacts of electricity price**	**Energy and Mining**	**2007**
105	Morocco	Housing (slum upgrading)	Urban Development	2005
106	Morocco	Water sector	Water Supply and Sanitation	2006
107	**Morocco**	**Water supply and sanitation (Phase 2); tariff reforms supported by water Development Policy Lending**[a]	**Water Supply and Sanitation**	**2007**
108	**Mozambique**	**Primary school fees reduction**	**Education**	**2004**
109	**Mozambique**	**Labor market**	**Public Sector Governance**	**2006**
110	Namibia	Extension and application of the Poverty Analysis Macroeconomic Simulator framework to Namibia	Economic Policy	2006
111	**Nepal**	**Fuel prices**	**Economic Policy**	**2005**
112	Nepal	Infrastructure	Transport	2005
113	Nicaragua	Public investment program (proposal was written for public sector management reform)	Public Sector Governance	2004
114	**Nicaragua**	**CAFTA**	**Economic Policy/Trade**	**2003**
115	**Nicaragua**	**Education for All**	**Education**	**2003**
116	**Nicaragua**	**Fiscal reform**	**Economic Policy**	**2003–04**
117	**Nicaragua**	**Water**	**Energy and Mining**	**2005**
118	Niger	Energy sector privatization	Energy and Mining	2004
119	Pakistan	Safety net review	Social Protection	2005
120	Pakistan	Education	Education	2005
121	Romania	Mining	Energy and Mining	2005

	Country	Reform	Sector classification	Fiscal year of funding
122	Rwanda	Tea sector privatization	Rural Sector	2003–04
123	**Rwanda**	**Poverty Analysis Macroeconomic Simulator modeling**	**Economic Policy**	**2005**
124	Senegal	Groundnut sector liberalization	Rural Sector	2004
125	Serbia	Welfare and labor impacts of mining sector	Energy and Mining	2005
126	**Serbia**	**Gender analysis of pension reform scenarios**	**Social Protection**	**2006**
127	**Sierra Leone**	**Mining sector**	**Energy and Mining**	**2005–06**
128	**Sierra Leone**	**Minimum wage policy**	**Economic Policy**	**2006**
129	Slovakia	Distributional impact of reform of tax and benefit system	Economic Policy	2007
130	Sri Lanka	Health expenditure business impact analysis	Health, Nutrition, and Population	2003
131	Sri Lanka	Agricultural trade policy and poverty reduction	Rural Sector	2006
132	**Sri Lanka**	**Land**	**Rural Sector**	**2005**
133	**Sri Lanka**	**Welfare—cash transfer scheme**	**Social Protection**	**2002**
134	Sudan	Increased public spending on health and education services and utilization by the poor in Northern Sudan	Health, Nutrition, and Population	2006
135	Sudan	Oil price increase and principles and options for compensation	Energy and Mining	2007
136	**Tajikistan**	**Energy**	**Energy and Mining**	**2006**
137	Tajikistan	Cotton farmland privatization	Rural Sector	2004
138	Tanzania	Local revenue	Public Sector Governance	2005–06
139	**Tanzania**	**Crop boards**	**Rural Sector**	**2004**
140	Tanzania	Low electricity tariffs for the rich	Energy and Mining	2007
141	Timor-Leste	Policy note on safety nets	Social Protection	2007
142	**Turkey**	**Labor market**	**Public Sector Governance**	**2003**
143	**Turkey**	**Social security**	**Social Protection**	**2004**
144	**Uganda**	**Land policy in northern Uganda and implications for resettlement and recovery**	**Rural Sector**	**2006**
145	**Uganda, Tanzania, Kenya**	**Local government tax reform in Uganda, Tanzania, and Kenya**	**Economic Policy**	**2006**
146	Ukraine	Fiscal decentralization	Public Sector Governance	2005
147	**Ukraine**	**Energy sector impact**	**Energy and Mining**	**2004**
148	**Ukraine**	**Health and education**	**Health, Nutrition, and Population**	**2005**
149	**Uruguay**	**Participatory monitoring (multisectoral Development Policy Lending)**	**Public Sector Governance**	**2006**
150	Venezuela, R. B. de	Poverty and social impact of the Misiones Initiative in Venezuela	Social Development	2006

(*continued on next page*)

	Country	Reform	Sector classification	Fiscal year of funding
151	Vietnam	Land reform	Public Sector Governance	2005
152	Vietnam	World Trade Organization accession	Economic Policy/Trade	2004
153	**Vietnam**	**Labor market impact of state-owned enterprise**	**Public Sector Governance**	**2002**
154	**Yemen, Rep. of**	**Energy sector analysis – social assessment/training**	**Energy and Mining**	**2003**
155	**Yemen, Rep. of**	**Water sector**	**Water Supply and Sanitation**	**2006**
156	Zambia	Land reform/titling; removal/reduction of fertilizer subsidy; rural roads	Rural Sector	2004

Sources: World Bank SDN and PREM Anchors.

Note: Bold entries are the 58 randomly sampled PSIAs. This list does not include the initial group of pilot PSIAs. CAFTA = Central America Free Trade Agreement; PSIA = poverty and social impact analysis.

a. As no documents were available for the then ongoing phase II of the Water Supply and Sanitation PSIA, the Phase I PSIA was assessed in the portfolio review instead.

This appendix contains a description of the methodology for each of the six evaluative instruments used in this study: the portfolio review, country case reviews, semistructured interviews with country stakeholders and Bank staff, interviews with senior Bank staff and managers, a thematic review of donor involvement in PSIAs, and a literature review.

I. Portfolio Review

To conduct a detailed desk review of PSIAs, a stratified random sample of the total universe was taken. Starting with the 156 PSIAs provided by the Bank's Poverty Reduction and Economic Management and Sustainable Development Network Anchors, and removing 16 PSIAs whose status was incomplete, a stratified, statistically representative, random sample of 58 PSIAs was taken of the remaining 140. Stratification was first by funding year then by network. The sample is significant at a 95 percent confidence interval at ±10 percent margin of error.

Information was then collected on these 58 PSIAs based on several factors: (i) the PSIA report or document itself (in some cases this was a chapter in a Bank economic and sector work [ESW] such as a Poverty Assessment); (ii) any funding proposals or progress reports available for the PSIA; (iii) a questionnaire sent to all task managers of the 58 PSIAs, for which there were responses for 37 PSIAs; (iv) project documents for PSIA-linked operations; (v) information recorded in the PSIA's file on Project Portal, when available; and (vi) any further relevant information provided by anchor staff. The information collected related to basic data on the PSIAs and their record in

fulfilling the Ten Elements of Good Practice PSIAs, as identified on the Bank's PSIA Web site and in the User's Guide. More specifically, the information gathered was the following.

Type
- PSIA document date and start date
- Description of focus of PSIA
- Was a specific policy reform analyzed? If not, then what type of study was it? (for example, background work)
- Was the PSIA a stand-alone piece or chapter/ section of another report?
- Was the PSIA multisectoral? If so, what other sectors were involved?

Inputs
- What activities were undertaken in the preparation stages of the PSIA?
- Was there a peer review of the PSIA concept note?
- Was there a peer review of previous PSIA drafts?
- Were there comments from other stakeholders on previous drafts of the PSIA?
- What was the skills mix of the study team?
- What was the study team's budget?
- How much time was allocated for the PSIA?
- Composition of study team authors
- Composition of overall study team

Element 1: Asking the Right Questions
- Why did the study team pick the topic for the PSIA?
- What were the PSIA's stated objectives?
- What was the timing of the PSIA regarding individual Bank operations?
- What was the timing of the PSIA in regard to policy implementation in the country?

Element 2: Identifying Stakeholders

- Did the PSIA identify the appropriate range of stakeholders who might be either beneficiaries or adversely impacted by the policy reform(s) supported by the PSIA?
- Were the distributional impacts on women and other traditionally vulnerable populations explicitly discussed? If not, was a justification offered for their exclusion?
- Were these stakeholders actually consulted during the course of the study?
- Given the nature of the reform, was the appropriate range of stakeholders who would affect the success of the policy implementation (that is, act as proponents or opponents of the reform) identified?
- Were these stakeholders actually consulted during the course of the study?

Element 3: Understanding Transmission Channels

- What transmission channels of the proposed reform (that is, employment, prices, access to goods and services, assets, and transfers and taxes) did the PSIA discuss?
- Did the PSIA highlight whether the impacts through these transmission channels would occur directly or indirectly?
- Did the PSIA specify whether the impact on stakeholders will differ between the short run and the long run?

Element 4: Assessing Institutions

- Did the PSIA consider how the structure of existing market and/or social institutions would mediate the impact of the proposed policy reform?
- Did the PSIA identify all the main agencies/institutions that are responsible for implementing the policy reform? If so, what specific aspects of these agencies/institutions were assessed (for example, responsibilities, incentives, capacity, accountability flows, or resource flows)?

Element 5: Gathering Data and Information

- Was the PSIA's data-collection approach most appropriate, given the nature of the reform being analyzed and the analytical tools being employed?

- If there were data limitations, how did the PSIA team overcome them to still analyze the reform's impact (collect more data, adapt the analytical approach, use "off-the-shelf" survey instruments, recommend a pilot study, and so forth)?
- If key data limitations existed, did the PSIA recommend a strategy to overcome them for future analyses of the poverty and social impact of the reform policy?

Element 6: Analyzing Inputs

- What quantitative tools were used in the study?
- What qualitative tools were used in the study?
- If high indirect impacts were expected, were the tools appropriate for capturing those impacts?

Element 7: Enhancement and Compensatory Measures

- Did the PSIA reveal that the proposed reform would have or did have adverse consequences for the poor or other groups?
- What were the policy recommendations?
- Were alternative policy options presented?
- Did the PSIA suggest altering the design of the policy to include complementary measures that would enhance the positive effects of the reform for the poor?
- Did the PSIA suggest altering the design of the policy to include complementary measures that would mitigate the negative effects of the reform for the poor?
- Did the PSIA suggest a compensatory mechanism for losers of the reform?
- If so, did the study discuss ways to design these mechanisms to ensure appropriate targeting of beneficiaries and to avoid distorting incentives that would compromise the reform's implementation?
- Did the PSIA recommend suspending the reform or delaying its implementation until a later period?
- Was there any prioritization of the policy recommendations?

Element 8: Assessing Risks

- Did the PSIA take into account risks to the reform program and/or risks emerging from the impact of the reform (for example, institutional risks, political economy risks, exogenous risks, or other country risks)?

- If so, did the PSIA incorporate these risks into its discussion of policy choices and policy design?

Element 9: Monitoring and Evaluation

- Did the PSIA suggest key indicators that should be collected ex ante to monitor and evaluate the reform's progress?
- Was a time frame suggested for how frequently these indicators should be updated?
- If key information was deemed necessary for monitoring and evaluating impacts but was unavailable at the time of the study, did the PSIA offer suggestions for how to fill this knowledge gap?
- Did the PSIA offer any recommendations for conducting a process evaluation to understand how and why the policy reform had a particular outcome?
- Did the PSIA suggest ways to implement a monitoring and evaluation system?

Element 10: Fostering Policy Debate and Feeding Back into Policy Choice

- When, how, and to whom was the PSIA disseminated?
- If another language besides English was widely spoken in the country, was the PSIA translated into that language?
- How well organized and written was the study?
- How operationally oriented were the findings (as opposed to being too academic/research oriented)?
- Did the PSIA discuss how lessons learned from implementing and evaluating the reform could be integrated into the policy process?

Impact: Bank operations

- Was the PSIA intended to inform a PRSC? If so, which one?
- Did the PRSC refer to the findings/recommendations of the PSIA?
- Was the PSIA intended to inform another DPL? If so, which one?
- Did the DPL document refer to the findings/recommendations of the PSIA?

- Was the PSIA intended to inform a Country Assistance Strategy (CAS)? If so, which one?
- Did the CAS refer to the findings/recommendations of the PSIA?
- Was the PSIA intended to inform an investment loan? If so, which one?
- Did the investment loan document refer to the findings/recommendations of the PSIA?
- Was the PSIA intended to inform an ESW? If so, which one?
- Did the ESW refer to the findings/recommendations of the PSIA?
- Was the PSIA intended to inform an additional ESW? If so, which one?
- Did the ESW refer to the findings/recommendations of the PSIA?
- Was the PSIA intended to inform any other operations/loans/strategies? If so, which ones?
- Did these additional operations/loans/strategies/documents refer to the findings/recommendations of the PSIA?
- Did Country Assistance Evaluations from the Independent Evaluation Group (IEG) mention the impact of the PSIAs?
- Did the IEG CAS Completion Report mention impact of the PSIAs?

Impact: Country policies

- Was the PSIA intended to inform a PRSP?
- If so, did the PRSP reflect the findings/recommendations of the PSIA?
- Even if the PSIA and supplementary documents did not indicate that the PSIA was to inform a PRSP, was there a PRSP available that it could inform? If so, which one? (This would only refer to PRSPs that were concurrent or subsequent to the start date of the PSIAs.)
- If there was a PRSP that the PSIA could inform, did that PRSP reflect the findings/recommendations of the PSIA?
- Was the PSIA intended to inform any other country policies?
- If so, did the policy document reflect the findings/recommendations of the PSIA?
- Was the PSIA focus country included in any IEG sector or thematic studies?
- If so, what did the study say about the impact of the PSIA?

II. Country Case Reviews

Eight countries were chosen purposively for Regional, sectoral, and fiscal year coverage: Bangladesh, Cambodia, Ghana, Malawi, Mali, Mozambique, Nicaragua, and Zambia. Within these countries, 12 PSIAs were examined in depth (see table C.1). The country case reviews involved visits to the countries concerned, except to Cambodia and Mali. In Cambodia and Mali, extensive interviewing of stakeholders was undertaken, significantly more than for the semistructured interviews with country stakeholders and Bank staff.

The country case reviews included an analysis of the effect of the PSIA on country policies and Bank operations and the contribution of the PSIA to country capacity for policy analysis. In countries where more than one PSIA was examined, the effect of each PSIA was reported on separately. To assess these three topics, the country case review examined the following elements.

Process and content of the PSIA

- What was the policy issue or problem that the PSIA addressed? Why was it important?

Were other donors active on the same issue?

- The roles of the Bank and the government in initiating and defining the focus of the PSIA. What were the main motives of each? (For instance, was the PSIA supposed to feed into a PRSP or into other analytic or policy choice exercises in the Bank and/or the government?)
- When and how was the PSIA carried out? How was responsibility divided/shared between government and the World Bank? Was there much/some/little consultation within the government, with nongovernment stakeholders, or with other donors (if appropriate)?
- What were the main findings and recommendations of the PSIA? Did it analyze policy alternatives? Did it identify risks of proposed policies? Did it suggest ways to buffer negative impacts and enhance positive ones?

Effect on country policies

- How much and what kind of effect did the PSIA have on government policies and actions and on the in-country policy debate? What is the

Table C.1: PSIAs Covered by the Country Case Reviews

Country	Reform	Sector classification	Fiscal year of funding
Bangladesh	Chittagong Port	Transport	2004
Cambodia	Rice tariffs	Economic Policy/Trade	2002
Cambodia	Social concessions of land reform	Social Development	2004
Ghana	Energy pricing and subsidies	Energy and Mining	2004
Malawi	Tobacco marketing	Rural Sector	2004
Malawi	Agriculture market closures	Rural Sector	2006
Mali	Cotton sector	Rural Sector	2004
Mozambique	Primary school fees reduction	Education	2004
Mozambique	Labor market	Public Sector Governance	2006
Nicaragua	Fiscal reform	Economic Policy	2003–04
Nicaragua	Water	Energy and Mining	2005
Zambia	Land reform/titling; removal/reduction of fertilizer subsidy; rural roads	Rural Sector	2004

Source: IEG.

evidence for this? If there had been no PSIA, what difference would that have made?

- Explanations for PSIA effect or lack thereof on the government.
- Good/bad practice examples and lessons learned.

Effect on the World Bank

- How much and what kind of effect did the PSIA have on World Bank decisions and operations? What is the evidence of this?
- If there had been no PSIA, what difference would that have made?
- Explanations for PSIA effect or lack thereof on the World Bank.
- Good/bad practice examples and lessons learned.

Contribution to country capacity

- How much and what kinds of impact did the PSIA have on the capacity of government agencies with regard to collecting and analyzing data on poverty, distributive impact, or other social effects of policies? Was there any impact on nongovernmental agencies, such as think tanks or universities?
- Did the PSIA have any impact on consultation and coordination among government agencies or with nongovernmental organizations?
- Explanations for PSIA impact or lack thereof on capacity.
- Good/bad practice examples and lessons learned.

Those interviewed were government officials in ministries and agencies responsible for the PSIA or within whose sector the PSIA fell, members of civil society organizations involved in the sector or subject matter covered by the PSIA, and staff of the World Bank and other donor agencies.

III. Semistructured Stakeholder Interviews with Country Stakeholders and Bank Staff

Semistructured telephone interviews were conducted with 47 stakeholders (9 government officials, 4 private sector representatives, 2 nongovernmental organization [NGO] staff, 11

academics and researchers, 2 officials from donor agencies, and 19 Bank staff) chosen purposively to include stakeholders familiar with the PSIA process. One stakeholder was interviewed on two PSIAs, resulting in a total of 48 stakeholder interviews. These interviews covered 11 PSIAs in 10 countries (and were additional to the ones covered in the country case reviews). The 11 PSIAs are listed in table C.2.

The topics covered in the interviews were as follows:

- Respondent's profile
- PSIA content and process
  - Initiation and choice of the PSIA topic
  - Timing
  - Soundness of conclusions
  - Participation
  - Dissemination
  - Donor involvement
- Effect on country policies/programs and on in-country analytical capacity
  - Accountability
  - Lesson learning
- Effect on World Bank
  - Accountability
  - Lesson learning

The results of these interviews are illustrative only and are not considered statistically representative.

IV. Interviews of Senior Bank Staff and Managers

Semistructured interviews were conducted with 30 senior Bank staff and managers (for example, country directors or advisors) chosen purposively for their knowledge of PSIAs.

The topics discussed included the following:

- Respondent involvement with PSIA
- Prominence of PSIAs in the Bank's Country program/dialogue
- Choice of PSIA topics
- Overall PSIA effectiveness
- PSIA work since termination of the Incremental Fund

Table C.2: PSIAs Covered by the Semistructured Interviews

Country	Short-hand name	Full PSIA title	Date of document
Albania	Irrigation and drainage reform	PSIA of the Irrigation and Drainage Rehabilitation projects and the Water Resource Management Project in Albania	2004
Armenia	Utility pricing and the poor	Utility Pricing and the Poor: Lessons from Armenia	2001
Benin	Cotton reform	Cotton Sector Reforms: A Poverty and Social Impact Analysis	2004
Egypt	Social policy reform	Egypt—Toward a More Effective Social Policy: Subsidies and Social Safety Nets	2005
Indonesia	Social protection reform	Chapter 6 of Indonesia Poverty Assessment: "Making Social Protection Work for the Poor"	2008
Indonesia	Macro reforms	Examining the Social Impact of the Indonesian Financial Crisis using a Macro-Macro Model	2002
Moldova	Energy sector reform	Sharing Power: Lessons learned from the Reform and Privatization of Moldova's Electricity Sector—Poverty and Social Impact Analysis	2004
Mongolia	Cashmere (trade)	From Goats to Coats: Institutional Reforming Mongolia's cashmere sector	2003
Nepal	Fuel prices	Nepal Poverty Assessment Background Paper: Socio Economic Impact of Fuel Prices in Nepal	2005
Sierra Leone	Minimum wage policy	Review of Civil Service Minimum Wage and Senior Executive Service Options	2006 (draft)
Sri Lanka	Land reform	Poverty and Social Impact Analysis (PSIA) of Sri Lanka's Land Policy Reforms, Socio-Economic Impact Assessment Final Report	2007

Source: World Bank.

- World Bank incentives for PSIA
- Long-term benefits from PSIA chapter in the Bank
- The future of PSIA work.

V. Thematic Review of Donor Involvement

The thematic review of donor involvement was conducted by means of a desk review of literature on and by donors actively supporting and conducting PSIAs and by interviewing 15 donor agency staff, World Bank staff, and other PSIA stakeholders about their experience with donor involvement in carrying out PSIAs.

VI. Literature Review

The literature review summarized findings of World Bank and other donor, NGO, and academic publications, policy notes, working papers, conference proceedings, and other relevant documents analyzing PSIA origins and record to date.

PSIA Effect on Country Policies

Bangladesh—Chittagong Port

The Chittagong Port Authority (CPA) has addressed some of the specific points from the PSIA that were incorporated in the January 2007 Bank Policy Note (World Bank 2007a). For instance, the CPA has taken actions to minimize the stuffing and unstuffing of containers and has increased container storage charges. However, the measures taken to date do not address the major recommendation of the PSIA (World Bank 2005e), which was to undertake a more comprehensive refiguring of the management structure of the port, which has not been acted on.

There was lack of engagement with key government bodies. Although the PSIA team got permission to undertake the study from the Ministry of Shipping and CPA, neither of those agencies participated in the design, analysis, or drafting of the PSIA. Moreover, because the Bank decided not to actively disseminate the report, it was not sent to the Ministry of Shipping or the Chittagong Port Authority for comment until one year and nine months after it was ready. Senior and long-standing officials interviewed in both organizations said they were not aware of such a study or its findings. Furthermore, the final report was also not shared at any stage with other stakeholders, including external partners, who may have been able to use the findings in some of their own interactions with the government.[1] Transparency International, the International Finance Corporation, and the Bangladesh Garment Manufacturers and Exporters Association were some of the groups that were eager to see the PSIA, even three years later.

The Bank has recently attempted to gauge the impact of the PSIA on government policy and has found some policy changes consistent with the PSIA's findings. However, there is insufficient evidence to attribute these policy changes to the PSIA. Overall, this PSIA had a moderate effect on country policies.

Cambodia—Rice Tariffs

There is no concrete evidence that the PSIA (ACI 2002) had an effect on the government of Cambodia's debates or policies. Although the Poverty Reduction Strategy (World Bank 2006c) mentions the need to increase agricultural productivity and improve access to inputs and credit and to improve infrastructure and the functioning of the financial system across the board, none of these points is brought up in the specific context of rice production or marketing, the topics of the PSIA; they are generic problems that are widely recognized in Cambodia. The agriculture section of the 2006 Poverty Reduction Strategy makes no mention of rice-specific reforms.

This lack of uptake is most likely due to (i) limited local ownership of the PSIA, (ii) limited involvement of local parties in analysis, (iii) the fact that this PSIA was not linked to a particular program proposal or reform, and (iv) lack of in-country Bank staff, who championed the report after completion. Overall, this PSIA had a negligible effect on country policies.

Cambodia—Social Concessions of Land Reform

Land reform was a key PRSP objective, and results from a PSIA on social land concession (World Bank 2004a) provided critical analytical inputs that helped implement this national priority. In particular, the PSIA sustained broad interest in and momentum around the land issue. The state land management subdecree of 2007 addressed many of the deficiencies of the prior land laws and was implemented after completion of the PSIA, although several years later. According to Bank and other interviewees, the process toward creation of the subdecree was fostered by the knowledge and consensus gained during the PSIA. This subdecree provided the necessary legal framework for identifying and managing land concessions at the local level. The PSIA identified clear problems with the existing legal framework and sustained movement toward resolution of these problems.

Furthermore, the PSIA helped build support within the government for a smallholder-based agricultural development scheme. Prior to 2003, many in government felt that efficiency in agriculture and investments in the sector would best be stimulated by supporting large-scale agricultural development. The economic concession program was one manifestation of this belief. In contrast, by focusing on potential impacts of smallholder development and identifying how smallholder agriculture could succeed, the PSIA helped change this perception and built subsequent support for a smallholder-based project, Land Allocation for Social and Economic Development (LASED), which received Bank financing.

This effect is due to several factors:

- The central importance of land reform to the Cambodian government contributed to the relevance of the PSIA and enabled its direct insertion into the national policy dialogue. The ex ante nature of the analysis and its timing relative to key policy decisions helped increase its relevance.
- The PSIA was very open about institutional weaknesses, particularly at the level of technical support units for local land use allocation committees. This information helped frame a clear path for successful implementation of the program. The PSIA also identified key weaknesses in enabling legislation and a lack

of clear guidance in the legal framework for local decision makers. These institutions were strengthened in subsequent years, partly as a result of the high profile the PSIA afforded these institutional weaknesses. The focus on institutions necessary for reform success assisted in stimulating further policy changes; prior to 2003, the government knew that additional legislation was needed (such as the 2007 subdecree) and the PSIA provided concrete guidance about elements of this legislation. The analysis also produced important information about complementary services and support needed to ensure that small-holder households would benefit following receipt of concession land. The government used this information in subsequent dialogue with donors about projects needed to support the social land concession program. The availability of complementary services, such as technical assistance, input supplies, marketing services, and so forth represents an essential component of reform sustainability.

- The inclusiveness of the process (with government, NGOs, and civil society participating) and the transparent, qualitative nature of the analysis won the confidence of the government. Very little (if any) of the analysis relied on abstract models or methods, and the simplicity of the analysis stimulated acceptance. Stakeholder participation was broad and active. The primary government partner, the Ministry of Land Management, Urban Planning, and Construction, was directly responsible for planning and implementing land policies; its participation built a strong institutional base of support within the government. The Ministry of Land Management, Urban Planning, and Construction was also engaged in the analysis of available land and, from this experience, was able to understand the multiple problems associated with identifying and quantifying such land. First-hand experience was invaluable. This ministry was engaged from the very start of the PSIA and continued its involvement through the end and beyond.

Overall, this PSIA had a substantial effect on country policies.

Ghana—Energy Pricing and Subsidies

A holistic study of the energy sources of the poor proposed by the PSIA (World Bank 2004e) has not been undertaken. Although there have been substantial improvements in access to electricity supplies, most of these improvements are attributed to the self-help program, which predated the PSIA. Arrangements for compound house dwellers remain unchanged. The recommended educational programs were not undertaken. Bank management reported that after the PSIA was completed, the Ministry of Finance opened a budget line for the lifeline subsidy—although the PSIA team expected this measure to help ensure that this subsidy would be paid, it recognized that this measure was not sufficient. The recommended system of monitoring was not implemented.

In large part, the lack of uptake of the recommendations may be caused by a lack of clear consensus within the government about the importance of the issues covered in the PSIA. There was also no natural counterpart on the Ghanaian side who would champion the report after its completion. Overall, this PSIA had a negligible effect on country policies.[2]

Malawi—Tobacco Marketing Reform

The tobacco PSIA (World Bank 2004h) advocated a wholesale overhaul of the legal and regulatory framework governing the sector, but little or no action has been taken to achieve this. The PSIA has not led to increased influence of the Malawian government or smallholder farmers in the trading of tobacco. The PSIA helped raise awareness among farmers about price setting processes and the government's pricing policy for tobacco, but the policy was unable to have an impact on buyer practices. Overall, this PSIA had a moderate effect on country policies.[3]

Malawi—Agriculture Market Closure

The analytical work contained in the PSIA (World Bank 2007c) has not had much effect on the measures taken by the Malawian government. The Malawi Agricultural Development and Marketing Corporation (ADMARC) has undergone some reorganization, but the proposed changes to the incentive system have not yet been realized. Although this PSIA dealt with these important issues, a longer-term process of follow-up to the findings and a careful analysis of the political economy surrounding ADMARC would be necessary to bring change. Overall, this PSIA had a negligible effect on country policies.[4]

Mali—Cotton Sector Reform

The PSIA work has not had much of an impact on government policy for several reasons. Because the government had already made its pricing decision in January 2005, when the PSIA was still in draft form, and because the PSIA does not engage with specific issues around the privatization of the Malian Textile Development Company, it is unclear what specific government policy the study could have informed. Although the draft PSIA might have been used by the Bank in its discussions with the government, a clear linkage between its findings and the government's ultimate pricing decision on cotton is not evident.[5]

A working paper primarily provides descriptive information and poverty estimates based on simulations and models that cannot easily be transformed into policy advice. The other outputs that have been generated from the PSIA work, including the poverty maps and 2006 survey data, highlight problems in the Sikasso region but stop short of identifying remedies and point to the need for complementary work. Furthermore, there has been a significant lag time between conducting the analysis and writing up the report, which is still not complete. The working paper also has not been held to a deadline; it has now been in the working stage for more than three years. Stakeholders have not received any draft since May 2006. Overall, this PSIA work has had a negligible effect on country policies.[6]

Mozambique—Primary School Fee Reduction

The qualitative findings reported earlier were one of the factors that influenced the government to abolish fees. The extensive information on supply- and demand-side factors influencing access as discussed in the PSIA (World Bank 2005h) has shaped government thinking on education. Many of its concerns regarding access to education by the most vulnerable members of society are echoed in the second strategic plan of education. Through the PSIA, government officials learned about the additional expenses parents pay when they send their children to school and the variation in access across districts. In addition, the government has a greater understanding of gender and education, as well as the particular challenges that orphans face regarding education.

The impact the draft PSIA had on the government can in part be explained by two factors: government support or buy-in, and auspicious timing. The PSIA was undertaken in collaboration with the Ministry of Education and, in particular, the National Institute for Educational Development, which participated extensively in the design, research, and analysis of the qualitative half of the study. This inclusiveness, which was most likely facilitated by the Ministry of Education's commitment to universal primary education, enabled uptake of the findings by government.

The timing of the PSIA also facilitated uptake, as the PSIA was being undertaken while the government was in the midst of developing an Education Sector Strategic Program for 2005–10. Overall, this PSIA had a substantial effect on country policies.

Mozambique—Labor Market Reform

The effect of the PSIA on government policy is not clearly attributable to the PSIA (World Bank 2006h). Aside from the recommendation on transitional provisions, there was little buy-in from the Ministry of Labor. The PSIA was undertaken at a time when a proposed reform to the labor law was already under consideration by the Council of Ministers. The mandate of the PSIA was also limited to comparing the previous and proposed labor laws, clarifying the major differences between the old policy and the new reform. It is likely that, regardless of the PSIA, the government would have passed the reform anyway.

The government had already negotiated with the private sector and the trade unions to change the labor law, had already done its own research,

and had already sent a draft law to Parliament. In addition, a new president, who owed his political support to organized labor, had just come into office, and it was highly unlikely that a study would have influenced the government's direction with regard to labor law reform. However, one of the very few recommendations that the report made was that if the government decided to revise the labor law, it should consider transition provisions to ease the impact of the reforms on existing workers. The government adopted this recommendation, and the draft labor law was amended to include generous transition arrangements for labor.

The PSIA provided limited actionable recommendations, most likely due to the high level of controversy surrounding the reform, the relatively late timing of the PSIA, and the involvement of the Ministry of Planning and Development but not the Ministry of Labor. Although the Ministry of Planning and Development did participate in the PSIA, the absence of the Ministry of Labor, under whose responsibility the new policy would fall, left a narrow channel for government uptake of the results. Overall, this PSIA had a moderate effect on country policies.

Nicaragua—Fiscal Reform

As an ex post assessment, the PSIA (World Bank 2003a) came too late to inform policy formulation, and it is difficult to discern what effect, if any, it had on the government. Judging by interviews with government officials, legislators, other Nicaraguans involved in the broader poverty-reduction strategy process, and representatives from the international donor community, the fiscal reform PSIA does not appear to have had much effect. Overall, this PSIA had a negligible effect on country policies.

Nicaragua—Water Reform

Despite the centrality of access to water in the poverty reduction strategy and the Millennium Development Goals, the water PSIA itself (World Bank 2005j) had little effect in government circles, either among those then in power or among those who succeeded them. The ideological tide was just about to turn, and the type of decentralization-cum-privatization of management/ownership of the water works that the PSIA advocated was totally at odds with the tenor of the soon-to-be administration. The last year of the administration was not a good time to tackle this controversial issue in Nicaragua.

Moreover, the PSIA, having been conducted by a third-country consultant and lacking participatory methods to engender domestic support, left no domestic constituency to lobby for the reform when the new administration came into power. Overall, this PSIA had a negligible effect on country policies.

Zambia—Land, Fertilizer, and Rural Roads

The findings of the PSIA (World Bank 2005l) did not directly inform subsequent government policy on land, fertilizer, and rural infrastructure.

Since the publication of the PSIA in 2005, the government has done little with regard to revising transport and land policies, although most government officials demonstrated awareness that these are important issues. The government has not implemented any new land or fertilizer initiatives; furthermore, it has not addressed the defects in the fertilizer support program. In fact, the abuses in the fertilizer support program have grown worse according to representatives of the U.S. Agency for International Development, Civil Society for Poverty Reduction, the European Union, and the National Farmers' Union.

In contrast, the government did not proceed with the draft land policy that the PSIA had criticized. Though no government official referenced the PSIA's effect on this issue, the PSIA task team hypothesized that the government's inaction on the land issue may have been informed by the report's findings. The PSIA's position on the draft land policy echoes the views of many of the civil society organizations that pressure the government. In that sense, it may have been one of the reasons the government did not proceed with the reform.

At first glance, the context of the PSIA appears to have been very favorable with regard to

shaping government policy. The government had a proposed land law that the PSIA analyzed in detail; the government was preparing a transport policy at that time that the section on rural infrastructure could have contributed to; and the fertilizer support program had been in place several years. The PSIA provided a useful assessment of the benefits and drawbacks of the program on which the government could have based a revised approach.

A number of reasons may explain why the report's findings were not more influential:

- Both the fertilizer program and the land issue are highly politicized. Since the final report came out in 2005, just one year prior to a general election, it is likely that the government preferred to maintain the status quo. The Fertilizer Support Program, the Food Security Pack, and maintaining customary land tenure practices were key instruments of the policy to win support from rural chiefs and residents in 2006. In fact, according to one agricultural specialist in the World Bank, the Zambian government raised the fertilizer subsidy level to 60 percent just before the 2006 election. This strategy was politically successful, as election results indicate that the ruling party gained 43 percent of the vote in 2006 from support from rural areas. Thus, fear of the consequences of changing agricultural subsidies or the land policy prior to the 2006 election help explain why the government did not adopt the recommendations on fertilizer and land in the PSIA.
- Since the PSIA was undertaken, copper prices have soared, offering an alternative source of revenue to agriculture. The government has therefore begun to turn its attention to renegotiating contracts and managing the impact of copper revenue, as has the Bank.
- According to many of the donors and civil society organizations interviewed, key local and national elites benefit from the subsidies in the fertilizer support program and from inaction on the land issue.
- In addition to the political climate and elite interest in the status quo, it is likely that some of

the content of the findings and the process of the report explain its limited effect. Regarding land, the report's recommendations disagreed with the government's policy position. Whereas the draft land policy proposed incorporating more land under state control, the PSIA sharply disagreed, noting the possible negative effects on the authority of chiefs, the weak capacity of the state to grant titles, and the possible negative impact on the poor if the state were to move to a system of individual titling.

- There is also the issue of which ministry was involved in the PSIA. Although the PSIA examined critical issues relating to rural agriculture, the Ministry of Agriculture and Cooperatives did not participate in or contribute to the PSIA. Instead, the Ministry of Finance and National Planning was the government sponsor of the study, perhaps because the PSIA was prepared in association with the Country Economic Memorandum. Because the Ministry of Agriculture and Cooperatives did not contribute to the study beyond consultations with individual project leaders, there was little ownership and little knowledge of the findings of the PSIA by this ministry.

Overall, this PSIA had a moderate effect on country policies.

PSIA Contribution to Country Capacity

Bangladesh—Chittagong Port
The PSIA team did not involve any other stakeholders in the design or preparation of the report. Overall, this PSIA (World Bank 2005e) had a negligible effect on country capacity, either in the government or outside.

Cambodia—Rice Tariffs
The Ministry of Agriculture, Forestry, and Fisheries guided the PSIA team, but there was little enhancement of their own capacity as a result of this PSIA (ACI 2002). Overall, this PSIA had a negligible effect on country capacity.

Cambodia—Social Concessions of Land Reform
Ministry staff participated in the analysis of available land, but because the PSIA (World Bank 2004a) did not accurately measure land availability, any learning-by-doing is likely to have been weak. Overall, this PSIA had a negligible effect on country capacity.

Ghana—Energy Pricing and Subsidies
In the Kumasi Institute of Technology and Environment, which was contracted as the local consultant for the PSIA (World Bank 2004e), considerable training inputs were provided by external consultants and the Bank team, and methods new to the Institute's personnel were introduced. The Institute's staff benefited from the training in qualitative research, and competence was further enhanced through continuous discussions and reviews.

The Electricity Company of Ghana also benefited in terms of capacity building from the energy PSIA (World Bank 2004e). It attached a member of its staff to the consultant teams that undertook the survey on which much of the energy PSIA report was based. As a result, the company learned a great deal about its customers, for example, regarding billing arrangements in compound houses. Four years on, and despite nonimplementation of its recommendations, the company continues to regard the energy PSIA as having had positive value, saying, "We now have the capacity and need to do more of such studies—but we don't have the funding."

Overall, this PSIA had a substantial effect on country capacity.

Malawi—Tobacco Marketing Reform
Three of the four papers that make up this PSIA (World Bank 2004h) were written by local policy analysts, including analysts in the Centre for Social Research of the University of Malawi and a Malawian consulting firm, O&M Development Consulting Ltd. However, there is little evidence that the Bank provided much training or enhanced the existing capacity of these agencies and, especially in the case of the value chain analysis in the PSIA, these technically more complicated components of the PSIA had less local input. Overall, this PSIA had a negligible effect on country capacity.

Malawi—Agriculture Market Closure

The ADMARC PSIA (World Bank 2003f) was partially conducted by local experts. Three background studies were prepared by staff of the Centre for Social Research of University of Malawi and by Wadonda Consulting. However, it is unclear if the existing capacity of these agencies was enhanced as a consequence of the PSIA. The more complicated quantitative components did not have local input, and capacity building was far less evident in government. Overall, this PSIA had a negligible effect on country capacity.

Mali—Cotton Sector Reform

The 2004 survey results, which the PSIA work analyzed, were administered with the help of a national research institute, but the analysis and write-up was done by Bank staff. One workshop in May 2005 offered a half-day session on cotton that included the results from a 2004 survey. A second workshop in February 2006 that lasted three days introduced the Social Accounting Matrix (SAM) tool and the SAM analysis of the cotton sector to Malian government officials, civil society, and donors. A final workshop, specifically devoted to the issues of cotton and poverty, was held in May 2006.

Although the SAM tool was developed by Bank staff, a workshop helped expose participants to how they could potentially use this new tool and highlight the links among different sectors of the Malian economy. The short length of the workshop, however, did not enable most participants to gain new analytic skills. Most participants were not able to use the SAM tool themselves but were appreciative of Bank staff efforts to show the capabilities of the tool. SAM was too technically sophisticated for most participants, and more intensive training would be required for participants to actually use the tool and fully understand the results. The Bank worked with the National Statistics Department on its survey, contributing to capacity development, but it is unclear if this was explicitly part of the PSIA on cotton. Overall, this PSIA work had a moderate effect on country capacity.

Mozambique—Primary School Fee Reduction

Partly as a result of the PSIA (World Bank 2005h), the Ministry of Education and Culture now appreciates the importance of including both qualitative and quantitative components, according to one former and one current official. Several members of the PSIA team gained experience using qualitative techniques such as interviewing and stakeholder analysis. In addition, team members developed some expertise with regard to survey design and implementation, and they report that they may now be able to do these types of studies in the future.

This moderate effect is likely due to the extensive participation of the Ministry of Education and the National Institute of Educational Development in the design, research, and analysis of the qualitative half of the PSIA. The fact that no locals were involved in the econometric analysis, however, is the likely reason for the lack of quantitative skill transfer. Overall, this PSIA had a moderate effect on country capacity.

Mozambique—Labor Market Reform

Although the Ministry of Planning and Development worked with Bank staff on this PSIA (Ministry of Planning and Development, Mozambique, and World Bank 2006), the experience of ministry staff with this PSIA highlights that they did not feel they had the mandate to comment on another ministry's (in this case, Labor) proposed reforms. That adversely affected the nature of their involvement and, consequently, the skill transfer. Overall, this PSIA had a negligible effect on country capacity.

Nicaragua—Fiscal Reform

The Ministry of Finance claims to have only a vague recollection of a fiscal PSIA study done by some foreign consultants a few years back and denies having learned any new technical skills; the ministry recognizes the possibility that a CD and a booklet or manual from someone at the World Bank may have been received.

Because this PSIA (World Bank 2003a) was conducted by a consulting firm and without substantial government involvement, it appears to have left no sustained increase in capacity. Overall, this PSIA had a negligible effect on country capacity.

Nicaragua—Water Reform

Given the limited scope and exposure of the water PSIA (World Bank 2005j) and the fact that it was carried out by a contracted external consultant, it is unlikely that it would have had much impact in expanding the country's analytical capacity. Overall, this PSIA had a negligible effect on country capacity.

Zambia—Land, Fertilizer, and Rural Roads

The PSIA (World Bank 2005l) does not appear to have contributed significantly to building country capacity, as there was little government participation. Some civil society organizations reportedly received training, but it was limited to several people. However, none of the civil society organizations contacted was able to confirm that any training had taken place.

Within the government, the lack of capacity development was most likely caused by the low levels of government participation. Although the Ministry of Finance and National Planning was said to be sponsoring the study and also supplied a cross-sectoral counterpart team to work with the PSIA team, government input was minimal. Beyond the initial consultations regarding the PSIA's area of focus, the government did not participate extensively in data gathering, analysis, or revision of the study. No government officials, departments, or ministries are cited among the PSIA authors or PSIA team participants. Overall, this PSIA had a negligible effect on country capacity.

PSIA Effect on Bank Operations

Bangladesh—Chittagong Port

The PSIA (World Bank 2005e) seems to have had some effect on World Bank analytical and advisory work, but not on Bank lending or strategy. Although some Bank staff say that the PSIA led them not to intervene in the port sector, others point to the uncertainties regarding political buy-in that were the reason for the lack of follow-up to the PSIA. The PSIA was not linked to a specific lending operation—neither the Export Infrastructure Development Program nor any of the Development Support Credits done after the PSIA.

Within the Bank, there was little collaboration between the social development unit in the Bank's South Asia Region, where the report was housed, and the transport sector in Washington, DC, which was responsible for port strategy. Key persons in the transport sector who dealt with port issues were not involved in the preparation of the report, nor was it shared with or disseminated to them directly. The lack of involvement or ownership by transport sector staff may explain why Bank sector work continued to push for privatization or why the recommendation for more radical reform was not taken forward. Sector staff, for instance, felt that the PSIA, which was an "anthropological" study, never translated into a project or technical assistance financing, as the Bank's transport program was stretched quite thin. The decision not to disclose the report publicly or even circulate it widely within the Bank resulted in it not being linked to a lending program or shared with other donors.[7]

However, within the Bank country team with whom the PSIA *was* shared, it was successful in encouraging more political economy analysis of reforms. Some Bank staff report that the PSIA created demand within the Bank in Bangladesh, and South Asia more generally, for conducting political economy analyses prior to designing or implementing policy advice. This kind of analysis was prominent in the CAS that followed, which notes that the Bank would reorient its processes to ensure a governance dialogue throughout project, analytical, and advisory activities preparation. For example, the CAS refers to a series of sector-specific political economy and governance studies that have been initiated, such as an upcoming study of the power sector. Overall, this PSIA had a moderate effect on Bank operations.

Cambodia—Rice Tariffs

It is possible that the PSIA (ACI 2002) influenced the Bank's general policy directions—the 2005 CAS, for example, mentions problems of a weak financial sector, poor infrastructure, and low rice productivity, all of which were identified in the PSIA—but there is no reference to the PSIA in the CAS, and interviewees were unable to confirm that the PSIA had any effect on World Bank thinking. Overall, this PSIA had a negligible effect on Bank operations.

Cambodia—Social Concessions of Land Reform

A major impact of the Cambodian land PSIA (World Bank 2004a) on the World Bank came through the PSIA's effect on the design of the Bank-supported LASED project. LASED benefited from the land PSIA in several ways. First, the PSIA yielded facts and information that reduced the cost and shortened the time involved in project preparation. For example, for information on identification of environmental concerns related to land transfer, partly as a result of the PSIA, LASED now contains specific provisions stating that land needs to be evaluated from an environmental perspective prior to its distribution.

Second, the PSIA informed the debate about the holding size necessary to meet food security needs of households; the current size of land concessions is now larger than it would have been in the absence of the PSIA. Third, approximately 25 percent of the project resources are now devoted to capacity building; this lack of capacity, particularly at the local level, was identified as a critical weakness in the PSIA. The remaining 75 percent of the resources are devoted to investment in communities; this investment is geared toward providing the infrastructure and supplementary services necessary to ensure that social land concessions succeed. These deficiencies were highlighted in the PSIA.

The PSIA also contributed to improving relationships between the World Bank and government, and the trust built during the process contributed to a smoother and more consensual project design.

This effect can be attributed to several factors:

- The analysis was well placed within the World Bank. In-country staff who were engaged in land-related programs were active participants in and promoted the PSIA. There was strong consultation between the PSIA team and staff designing the Bank operation and consultation between Regional staff and central network anchor staff. This helped ensure that the product was useful to their needs. Their interest contributed to a more lasting impact for the PSIA.

- The focus on elements of a successful reform program, on quantifying landlessness and on identifying complementary services, helped frame subsequent World Bank programs. The PSIA identified several risks and challenges related to social land concessions, such as the need for complementary services. These complementary services and investments form a key component of LASED. The focus on institutional weaknesses also informed subsequent Bank programs.

- The inclusiveness of the process helped increase influence within the Bank as staff recognized the usefulness of consultation and were glad to support a project that built goodwill with the government of Cambodia, donors, and civil society.

However, the relatively weak use of quantitative techniques may have limited some of the uptake in the Bank. In particular, the PSIA never measured potential impacts of the program, mainly because of inadequate data. Overall, this PSIA had a substantial effect on Bank operations.

Ghana—Energy Pricing and Subsidies

The energy PSIA (World Bank 2004e) had little effect on the Bank's CAS, successive PRSC loans, or important ESW then under way. Though the Energy Development and Access Project addressed issues of disparities in access to electricity, it did not substantially reflect the approaches supported by the PSIA in terms of special provisions for the poor in scaling-up access. The project did include some support for off-grid solar photovoltaic schemes, but this was not a focus area of the PSIA.[8]

The PSIA's limited effect within the Bank came from differences in approach between those responsible for the PSIA and those responsible for Bank energy interventions. Most energy specialists in the Bank did not include the issues of PSIA among their main priorities. No one in Washington or Accra had responsibility for promoting the messages of the report once it was produced, as was illustrated by a low awareness of the report within the Accra office. Overall, this PSIA had a negligible effect on Bank operations.

Malawi—Tobacco Marketing Reform

The program document for the First Poverty Reduction Support Grant to Malawi refers directly to the tobacco PSIA (World Bank 2004h) as a key analytical underpinning and states that, along with a previous study, "The PSIA identified several weaknesses in current marketing and institutional arrangements for tobacco, which hinder the efficiency of the sector and limit the pass-through of international prices to smallholders."

The PSIA's successful input into a Bank operation may be linked to its contribution in identifying a policy hurdle. Furthermore, this effect may have been facilitated by good communication between the PSIA team and Regional Bank staff. Overall, this PSIA had a substantial effect on Bank operations.

Malawi—Agriculture Market Closure

The program document for the First Poverty Reduction Support Grant to Malawi refers directly to the ADMARC PSIA (World Bank 2007c) as a key analytical underpinning, stating that the component of the PRSC program on improving the functioning of agricultural markets benefited from the PSIA on ADMARC reforms.

The PSIA's successful input into a Bank operation may be linked to its being carried out by Regional staff. Overall, this PSIA had a substantial effect on Bank operations.

Mali—Cotton Sector Reform

The PSIA's contribution has been to provide data on cotton-producing households and the SAM model that shows how various pricing structures affect poverty in producers' households. Some of the PSIA's findings are referenced in Structural Adjustment Credit IV and Poverty Reduction Support Credit 1, but these operations are not anchored by the PSIA work. According to Bank management, the PSIA informed the Bank's position on cotton prices. Overall, this PSIA work had a moderate effect on Bank operations.

Mozambique—Primary School Fee Reduction

There has been no Bank lending in the primary (or secondary) education sectors during or after this PSIA (World Bank 2005h), nor is this PSIA reflected in any analytical work. Overall, this PSIA had a negligible effect on Bank operations.

Mozambique—Labor Market Reform

The PSIA on labor (World Bank 2006h) has had a limited impact on Bank operations. With regard to its effect on Bank staff, it appears to have been largely ineffective. Most Bank staff who were not part of the core team expressed dissatisfaction with the quality of the report. They said that it did not assess the shortcomings of the new law or examine alternatives, that it lacked data and made claims it could not support, and that it did not clearly identify the beneficiaries and those adversely affected by the proposed reform. Overall, this PSIA had a negligible effect on Bank operations.

Nicaragua—Fiscal Reform

Even though the PRSC-I did not contain any explicit tax conditionality, the PSIA (World Bank 2003a) was referenced in the PRSC's analytic section, and the PRSC did stress the need to improve the administration and collection of taxes and improve the allocation and focus of social expenditure—both of which were consistent with the PSIA findings and recommendations. Overall, this PSIA had a substantial effect on Bank operations.

Nicaragua—Water Reform

Involvement in the PSIA (World Bank 2005j) may have weighed in the Bank's decision to raise its level of engagement in the water sector, as reflected in the Bank's subsequent Country Partnership Strategy for Nicaragua, which allocates $80 million to the sector over the 2008–12 timeframe. However, there is no clear attribution of this change to the PSIA in those documents. The Country Partnership Strategy does not even mention the water PSIA, though it does mention others. Overall, this PSIA had a moderate effect on Bank operations.

Zambia—Land, Fertilizer, and Rural Roads

Apart from the section on rural infrastructure, the substance of the PSIA (World Bank 2005l) did not inform Bank operations. A Bank-financed project to support commercial smallholders, by providing extension services and making other investments, was conceptualized before the PSIA was completed and was not informed by the PSIA findings. The report's recommendations regarding subsidies and titling were controversial within the Bank. The PSIA was prepared in association with the Country Economic Memorandum, but the PSIA and memorandum differed regarding the emphases they placed on the growth of a private sector in agriculture, the impact of land titling on the poor and the vulnerable, and the benefit and drawbacks of fertilizer subsidies and the stress they placed on market solutions for farmers in remote areas.

One further reason for limited effect is ownership, but this time on the part of the Bank. Because there was relatively minor input from in-country Bank staff and the funding came from a trust fund instead of the Regional budget, there was a lack of ownership of this PSIA among the Bank's operational staff. Overall, this PSIA had a negligible effect on Bank operations.

Money changer on bank of Senegal River. Photo by Scott Wallace, courtesy of the World Bank Photo Library.

APPENDIX E: SEMISTRUCTURED STAKEHOLDER INTERVIEWS—
SUMMARY OF RESULTS

Semistructured telephone interviews were conducted with 47 stakeholders (9 government officials, 4 private sector representatives, 2 NGO staff, 11 academics and researchers, 2 officials from donor agencies, and 19 Bank staff) chosen to include stakeholders familiar with the PSIA process. These interviews covered 11 PSIAs in 10 countries (and were additional to the ones covered in the country case reviews: Albania, Armenia, Benin, Egypt, Indonesia (two PSIAs), Moldova, Mongolia, Nepal, Sierra Leone, and Sri Lanka. Applying the same criteria as was applied to the country case reviews, the semistructured interviews indicated the following effect of PSIAs on country policies, country analytic capacity, and Bank operations. There was a high proportion of missing information for country analytic capacity—23 of the 48 stakeholder interviews yielded no assessment of this dimension. One stakeholder was interviewed on two PSIAs (in Indonesia), resulting in a total of 48 stakeholder interviews.

Table E.1: Summary of Semistructured Stakeholder Interviews

	Substantial	Moderate	Negligible	Unable to assess
Effect on country policies	10	24	11	3
Contribution to country analytic capacity	4	9	12	23
Effect on Bank operations	7	11	13	17

Source: IEG.

Indian girl. Photo by Curt Carnemark, courtesy of the World Bank Photo Library.

The data in this appendix are based on a review of the statistically significant random sample of 58 PSIAs selected out of the universe of 156 PSIAs.[1] The sources for the review of these 58 PSIAs are the PSIA report or document itself (in some cases a chapter in a Bank ESW such as a Poverty Assessment); any funding proposals or progress reports available for the PSIA; a questionnaire sent to all task managers of the 58 PSIAs, of which responses were received for 37 PSIAs; project documents for PSIA-linked operations; information recorded in the PSIA's file on Project Portal, when available; and any further relevant information provided by anchor staff, such as additional budget information. To minimize judgment effects, data classification was subject to a second-order review.

Table F.1: Did the PSIA Explicitly State Operational Objectives?

Operational objective[a]	Incidence[b] from portfolio review (excluding task manager questionnaire responses)	Incidence[b] (from task manager questionnaire responses conducted ex post of the PSIA)
Inform country policies and/or debate	41 (71%)	28 (76%)
Increase country capacity for policy analysis	7 (12%)	18 (49%)
Inform Bank operations	8 (14%)	20 (54%)
All of the above objectives stated	0 (0%)	12 (32%)
None of the objectives not explicitly stated	13 (22%)	—

Source: Portfolio review.
Note: N = 58 for column 1, and N = 37 for column 2. PSIA = Poverty and Social Impact Analysis.
a. Only explicitly stated operational objectives are taken into account.
b. Most PSIAs list more than one objective, so the percentages add up to more than 100 percent.

Table F.2: Did the PSIA Use Quantitative and/or Qualitative Methods?

Methodology used	Incidence
Quantitative analysis only	25 (43%)
Qualitative analysis only	4 (7%)
Both methods used	28 (48%)
Unknown	1 (2%)

Source: Portfolio review.
Note: The tally for PSIAs that used both methods includes any occurrence in which both a quantitative and qualitative instrument was used but does not attempt to assess the extent to which (if at all) these were done in tandem or influenced each other. N = 58. PSIA = Poverty and Social Impact Analysis.

Table F.3: Did the PSIA Identify Stakeholders?

	Incidence
a. Did the PSIA identify beneficiaries or those adversely affected by the reform?	
Explicitly identified beneficiaries or those adversely affected	20 (35%)
No explicit identification of beneficiaries or those adversely affected, but data or results disaggregated[a]	29 (51%)
No discussion or disaggregation of beneficiaries or those adversely affected	8 (14%)
b. Did the PSIA identify proponents or opponents of the reform?	
Yes	24 (42%)
No[b]	33 (58%)

Source: Portfolio review.
Note: The Rwanda Poverty Analysis Macroeconomic Simulator training is not included, so N = 57, not 58. PSIA = Poverty and Social Impact Analysis.
a. In these cases, the text of the PSIA did not discuss or identify beneficiaries or those adversely affected, but data used and/or presented in the analysis was disaggregated in some way (for example, poor vs. non-poor, urban vs. rural, consumers vs. producers).
b. Some of these did identify beneficiaries or those adversely affected, but only those that analyzed whether these groups would be proponents or opponents of the reform/policy are tallied here.

Table F.4: Did the PSIA Identify Institutions?

	Yes	Somewhat	No
Did the PSIA identify which institution(s) would be responsible for implementing the reform?	21 (37%)	14 (24%)	22 (39%)

Source: Portfolio review.
Note: The Rwanda Poverty Analysis Macroeconomic Simulator training is not included, so N = 57, not 58. PSIA = Poverty and Social Impact Analysis.

Table F.5: Did the PSIA Analyze Risks?

	Yes	No
Did the PSIA take into account institutional or other risks to implementing the reform program (or in the case of background work PSIAs, risks posed by current policies)?[a]	37 (65%)	20 (35%)

Source: Portfolio review.

Note: The Rwanda Poverty Analysis Macroeconomic Simulator training is not included, hence N = 57 not 58. PSIA = Poverty and Social Impact Analysis.

a. Risks to implementation include institutional capacity risks, political economy risks (for example, interest groups opposing reform), market risks (for example, weak credit markets, exogenous price shocks), weather risks (drought), and so forth.

Table F.6: Did the PSIA Incorporate Monitoring and Evaluation?

	Yes	No
Did the PSIA suggest key indicators or a data collection method necessary for monitoring and evaluation of the reform, policy, or sector?	16 (28%)	41 (72%)
Did the PSIA suggest ways of implementing an M&E system?	10 (18%)	47 (82%)

Source: Portfolio review.

Note: Although some PSIAs did call for a monitoring and evaluation system to be created, only those that gave recommendations for indicators, data collection, a methodology, or other plan of action were tallied. The Rwanda Poverty Analysis Macroeconomic Simulator training is not included, so N = 57, not 58. PSIA = Poverty and Social Impact Analysis.

Table F.7: Did the PSIA Involve Stakeholder Participation?

Type of activity	PSIAs that included activity
Focus groups/group interviews/stakeholder interviews/participatory rural appraisal/ workshops/forums, etc.	32 (56%)
No consultations mentioned with stakeholders	21 (37%)
Unclear or not applicable	4 (7%)

Source: Portfolio review.

Note: The Rwanda Poverty Analysis Macroeconomic Simulator training is not included, so N = 57, not 58. The PSIA was judged to have incorporated stakeholder participation if it explicitly mentioned focus groups, group interviews, stakeholder interviews, participatory rural appraisal, workshops, forums, and so forth with individuals and/or groups who would have been positively or adversely affected by the reform or regarded as proponents or opponents of the reform. PSIA = Poverty and Social Impact Analysis.

Table F.8: At What Stage Was the PSIA Disseminated?

	Number
Concept paper	15 (41%)
Background work	14 (38%)
Draft report	28 (76%)
Final report	22 (60%)

Source: Task manager questionnaires.

Note: N = 37. PSIA = Poverty and Social Impact Analysis.

Table F.9: What Form Did Dissemination Take?

Type of dissemination activity	Number of PSIAs that included activity
PSIA findings shared with government	32 (55%)
PSIA findings shared with civil society/NGOs	20 (35%)
Workshop held	19 (33%)
Dissemination to in-country sector specialists	2 (3%)
Report publicly available (Bank website)	23 (40%)
Dissemination activities planned, but no information on if they materialized	11 (19%)
No evidence of dissemination	12 (21%)
Not applicable[a]	3 (5%)

Source: Portfolio review.
Note: N = 58. PSIA = Poverty and Social Impact Analysis.
a. The PSIA is a chapter of another report, so dissemination of the PSIA work itself is impossible to track.

Table F.10: Where English Is Not Widely Spoken, Was There a Translation of the PSIA into the Local Language?

Yes	24 (60%)
No	16 (40%)

Source: Portfolio review.
Note: N = 40 because no information is available for the rest of the PSIAs, or English was widely spoken in the concerned countries. PSIA = Poverty and Social Impact Analysis.

Table F.11: How Many PSIAs Are Available on the Internet?

Is the PSIA on the Internet?	Number
Yes	33 (58%)
No	24 (42%)

Source: Portfolio review.
Note: PSIA = Poverty and Social Impact Analysis.

Table F.12: Did the Study Team Include a Local Organization or Researcher(s)?

Yes	41 in total[a] (71%)
Local consultants or researchers	30 (73%)
Local NGOs	3 (7%)
Government ministries/agencies	14 (34%)
No	10 (17%)
Information unavailable	7 (12%)

Source: Portfolio review.
Note: The "study team" includes those who were involved in any part of the PSIA process, beyond supplying pre-existing data, as noted in the PSIA itself, the task manager questionnaire, or PSIA progress report. N = 58. NGO = nongovernmental organization; PSIA = Poverty and Social Impact Analysis.
a. Totals more than 41 because some PSIAs included local organizations or researchers in more than one of the above categories.

Table F.13: What Was the Incidence of Peer Review?

	Yes	No/no indication
Was the PSIA Concept Note peer reviewed?	23 (40%)	34 (60%)
Was a draft of the PSIA peer reviewed?	30 (53%)	27 (47%)

Source: Portfolio review.
Note: The Rwanda Poverty Analysis Macroeconomic Simulator training is not included, so N = 57, not 58. PSIA = Poverty and Social Impact Analysis.

Woman from Mali. Photo courtesy of the World Bank Photo Library.

Management Response

1. IEG notes that its evaluation supports flexibility and recognizes that "[t]he 2008 PSIA Good Practice Note is an improvement over the 2004 PSIA Good Practice Note in that it grants considerable flexibility to the Regions… This flexibility will allow the scope and content of the PSIA to be better tailored to the specific context…."

2. IEG notes that the evaluation recognizes the evolution and refinement of the guidance materials. The evaluation covers PSIAs conducted over fiscal 2002–07 and includes evidence from interviews of Bank staff conducted in fiscal 2009, which point to the persistence of key problems such as lack of buy-in from operational staff and lack of understanding of what the PSIA approach is.

3. http://siteresources.worldbank.org/INTPSIA/ Resources/GPN_August08_final.pdf.

Chapter 1

1. Management notes that in the late 1990s and early 2000s, the Bank was in the process of reforming its policy governing adjustment lending (OP 8.60) and over the course of the year 2000 prepared a report, "Adjustment Lending Retrospective" (World Bank 2001a, pp. 25–45), that served as background for the update of the adjustment lending policy and its conversion to an Operational Policy/Bank Procedures (OP/BP) format. The poverty and social focus of adjustment lending was analyzed at length and in a candid way in that report, including the distributional effects of adjustment programs.

2. Management notes that the 156 PSIAs reflect mainly those financed by trust funds or stand-alone pieces of distributional analysis; these do not include all the poverty, social, and distributional impact analysis embedded in other World Bank ESW (such as Poverty Assessments, Public Expenditure Reviews, and gender and social assessments). IEG notes that these 156 PSIAs were the only ones identified as PSIAs by Bank management and provided to IEG.

3. A consortium of NGOs developed several criticisms in a paper entitled "Blind Spot: The Continued Failure of the World Bank and IMF to Fully Assess the Impact of Their Advice on Poor People" (Oxfam International and others 2007). These criticisms are that the Bank does not do enough PSIA, that it does not do enough to build country capacity or to foster country ownership, that there is insufficient disclosure of PSIA results by the Bank, and that PSIA focuses too much on mitigating the impacts of a predetermined reform and not enough on analyzing alternative policy options.

4. IDA deputies at the fourth IDA-15 replenishment meeting in November 2007 "encouraged management to strengthen the preparation of country and sector strategies and improve the conduct of poverty and social impact assessments" (World Bank 2007b).

5. Management notes that all three World Bank reports—the Development Policy Operations Retrospective, Assessing the use of Poverty and Social Impact Analysis in World Bank Development Policy Loans, and PSIA—Reviewing the Link to In-Country Policy and Planning Processes—will be completed by early fiscal 2010. The Development Policy Operation Retrospective has been prepared by Operations Policy and Country Services once every two years—reviewing the Bank's experience with Development Policy Operations, including compliance with aspects of OP 8.60 that relate to poverty and social impact analysis but not intended as a comprehensive self-evaluation of PSIA.

6. Management notes that, although supporting capacity development in this area, as in almost all areas of Bank assistance, is important, it was never the primary objective of PSIA work. IEG notes that this evaluation does not refer to capacity building as the "primary" objective of PSIAs and that the Bank's

2004 Good Practice Note states "…the Bank and other development partners have a major role in building local capacity for PSIA" (World Bank 2004f, para. 4). Furthermore, it also states, "Countries may require substantial support from the Bank and other development partners to carry out PSIA. Building an in-country constituency and capacity for PSIA will strengthen country ownership and increase the prospects for mainstreaming PSIA work" (para. 11).

Chapter 2

1. Management notes that IEG did not share its classification of individual pieces of PSIA work. As a result, management is unable to comment on the accuracy or relevance of the IEG categorizations or ratings in this chapter or in chapters 3 and 4 and appendix F. IEG notes that it offered management the data on which the classification is based, including PSIA reports, trust fund proposals, and task manager survey results, and offered to meet with Bank management to review how a subset of the PSIAs had been classified. IEG also clarifies that these classifications are relevant to only one paragraph in each chapter.

2. "N" here is 57 PSIAs and not 58, because the Rwanda PAMS training PSIA (World Bank 2007h) is excluded.

3. Management notes that in some cases, however, a general sector analysis is essential for devising different options for reform. Offering different options for reform, as opposed to evaluating the likely impact of a specific reform, is an important role that PSIA can play, depending on the country, sectoral context, and country demand. General sectoral analysis would be relevant for PSIA in such cases.

4. The assessment is made in general terms and does not differentiate between the reports that should have used a quantitative approach and those that should have used a qualitative or a combined mixed-methods approach.

5. The 60 percent figure includes the "somewhat" category; see appendix table F.4.

6. The PSIA was judged to have incorporated stakeholder participation if it explicitly mentioned focus groups, group interviews, stakeholder interviews, participatory rural appraisal, workshops, forums, and so forth with individuals and/or groups that would have been positively or adversely affected by the reform or regarded as proponents or opponents of the reform.

Chapter 3

1. Although the PSIA is on the Bank's external Web site (World Bank 2005e), this fact is not widely known and the Bank has not made efforts to actively disseminate it. Transparency International, staff in the International Finance Corporation, and the Bangladesh Garment Manufacturers and Exporters Association were among the groups that were interested in the PSIA but unaware of its availability.

2. Management notes that the unique political circumstances in which the PSIA was undertaken led to the management decisions on consultation and dissemination.

3. Management notes that the assessment of a negligible contribution to county analytic capacity is made in general terms and does not take into account whether capacity building was one of the stated objectives of the PSIA.

4. Management notes that IEG did not share its classification of individual pieces of PSIA work. As a result, management is unable to comment on the accuracy or relevance of the IEG categorizations or ratings in this chapter or in chapters 3 and 4 and appendix F. IEG notes that it offered management the data on which the classification is based, including PSIA reports, trust fund proposals, and task manager survey results, and offered to meet with Bank management to review how a subset of the PSIAs had been classified. IEG also clarifies that these classifications are relevant to only one paragraph in each chapter.

Chapter 4

1. Management notes that poverty and social and distributional analysis is not meant to be a "formal" practice across the Bank, but rather a set of tools used in stand-alone reports and integrated into regular ESW products, such as Poverty Assessments, Public Expenditure Reviews, gender assessments, and Country Economic Memoranda.

2. Management notes that IEG did not share its classification of individual pieces of PSIA work. As a result, management is unable to comment on the accuracy or relevance of the IEG categorizations or ratings in this chapter or in chapters 3 and 4 and appendix F. IEG notes that it offered management the data on which the classification is based, including PSIA reports, trust fund proposals, and task manager survey results, and offered to meet with Bank management to review how a subset of the PSIAs had been classified.

IEG also clarifies that these classifications are relevant to only one paragraph in each chapter.

3. Management notes that the supporting material in the paragraph highlights several PSIAs for which the operational staff had issues with the content or coverage. This does not support a "striking finding." There is often debate within the Bank on the coverage of analytical work, and that is healthy.

4. Management notes that, although there was a time at the start of the Ghana work when a change in energy unit task managers plus a heavy work load may have led to less than full engagement, over the medium term the energy unit did use the results of the PSIA, notably in informing the Ghana Energy Development and Access Project.

5. Management notes that the Good Practice Note (World Bank 2008b) reflects corporate guidance to staff on what the PSIA approach encompasses and indicates that PSIA is a set of analytical tools and methods that does not lend itself to universal standards, given the range of potential issues and the variety of methods needed for such analysis.

Appendix A

1. Management notes that in the late 1990s and early 2000s, the Bank was in the process of reforming its policy governing adjustment lending (OP 8.60) and prepared over the course of the year 2000 a report, Adjustment Lending Retrospective (World Bank 2001a), that served as background for the update of the adjustment lending policy and its conversion to an Operational Policy/Bank Procedures (OP/BP) format. The poverty and social focus of adjustment lending was analyzed at length and in a candid way in that report, including the distributional effects of adjustment programs (see pp. 25–45).

Appendix B

1. The list of 156 Bank-funded PSIAs over fiscal 2002–07 was identified by the Bank's PREM and SDN Anchors.

Appendix D

1. Management notes that the unique political circumstances in which the PSIA was undertaken led to the management decisions on consultation and dissemination.

2. Management notes that the government was very much engaged, including key decision makers, in select-ing the topic, monitoring production, and discussing its findings. There were extensive consultations with key decision makers, including chairing of the PSIA steering committee by the Minister of Energy; identification of the PSIA with the Ministry of Finance and Economic Planning; consultation with the multistakeholder steering committee on the Terms of Reference, on the selection of the firm, on the draft report, and on the findings through numerous meetings. In addition, it should be noted that after the PSIA work, the Ministry of Finance and Economic Planning included a discrete budget line for a lifeline subsidy.

3. Management disagrees with this analysis. Significant changes have been introduced, directly influenced by the tobacco PSIA. The governing legislation and regulatory framework for tobacco institutions were amended, resulting in strengthened representation of tobacco farmers on the Tobacco Control Commission Board. Several levies were also reduced substantially, resulting in increased returns to farmers. Four satellite auction floors were also opened to bring markets closer to farmers, resulting in further reductions in marketing costs. The Malawi government has become notably more interventionist in the trading of tobacco since the PSIA, although this was not the recommendation of the PSIA. The government's continued policy of setting minimum prices, which was also not recommended by the PSIA, has had a substantial impact on buyer practices but is likely seriously undermining the viability of the sector in the medium term.

4. Management disagrees with this analysis. The PSIA informed substantial changes in the scope and role of ADMARC, including the transfer of ADMARC warehousing assets to a separate company for subsequent lease to the private sector, which is continuing. As noted, this is a longer-term process that is currently being supported in a programmatic fashion by a Bank Poverty Reduction Support Credit series.

5. Management notes that, in fact, there were several meetings held in 2004 on issues of cotton pricing. Additionally, the results of the PSIA were a key input in informing dialogue with government on the need to undertake price reforms and were also used in several Development Policy Operations from 2004 onwards.

6. Management notes that the team working on the PSIA advised and helped the Mali Statistical Office put in its national survey for the first time a module

on income that will specifically allow analysts to distinguish the distributional impact of cotton price changes on incomes of producers versus other groups.

7. Management notes that the unique political circumstances in which the PSIA was undertaken led to the management decisions on consultation and dissemination.

8. Management notes that the statement that the PSIA had little effect on the power sector credit is inaccurate; the Ghana Energy Development and Access Project was influenced by the PSIA, specifically in the component that provides for low-cost energy solutions, including off-grid sources, that will benefit the northern populations. IEG notes that the PSIA specifically states that analysis of off-grid energy sources was beyond its scope. The PSIA states, "This includes analysis of pricing, access and efficiency of biomass fuels and kerosene, as well as exploration of alternative energy sources or off-grid energy sources for rural areas. Though these issues are beyond the scope of this PSIA, they merit further examination in subsequent research" (World Bank 2004e, p. xvii).

Annex F

1. Management notes that IEG did not share its classification of individual pieces of PSIA work. As a result, management is unable to comment on the accuracy or relevance of the IEG categorizations or ratings in this chapter or in chapters 3 and 4 and appendix F. IEG notes that it offered management the data on which the classification is based, including PSIA reports, trust fund proposals, and task manager survey results and offered to meet with Bank Management to review how a subset of the PSIAs had been classified. IEG also clarifies that these classifications are relevant to only one paragraph in each of chapters 3 and 4.

ACI (Agrifood Consulting International). 2002. "Rice Value Chain Study: Cambodia." World Bank Report, ACI, Bethesda, MD.

Angel-Urdinola, Diego, and Quentin Wodon. 2007. "Assessing the Targeting Performance of Social Programs: Cape Verde." In *Public Finance for Poverty Reduction: Concepts and Case Studies from Africa and Latin America,* ed. Blanca Moreno-Dodson and Quentin Wodon, 417–40. Washington, DC: World Bank.

C3 Management and Economic Consulting. 2006. "Review of Civil Service Minimum Wage and SES Options." Final report to Government of Sierra Leone, C3 Management, London.

Do, Quy-Toan, and Lakshmi Iyer. 2003. "Land Rights and Economic Development: Evidence from Vietnam." Policy Research Working Paper 3120, World Bank, Washington, DC.

IEG (Independent Evaluation Group). 2009. *Climate Change and the World Bank Group. Phase I: An Evaluation of World Bank Win-Win Energy Policy Reforms.* Washington, DC: World Bank.

———. 2008. *Using Knowledge to Improve Development Effectiveness: An Evaluation of World Bank Economic and Sector Work and Technical Assistance, 2000–2006.* Washington, DC: World Bank.

Ministry of Planning and Development, Mozambique, and World Bank. 2006. "Job Creation in Mozambique: Is Labor Law Reform the Answer?" World Bank, Washington, DC.

ODI (Overseas Development Institute) and World Bank. 2009. "Poverty and Social Impact Analysis: Reviewing the Link with In-Country Policy and Planning Processes." Draft synthesis report, World Bank, Washington, DC.

Oxfam International. 2000. "PRSPs and Poverty Impact Assessments: Letter to Mr. J.D. Wolfensohn and Mr. H. Köhler." Overseas Development Institute, London, 22 December.

Oxfam International, Save the Children U.K., CAFOD, Christian Aid, New Rules for Global Finance, Water Aid, Eurodad, TRICAIRE, Bretton Woods Project, and Norwegian Church Aid. 2007. "Blind Spot: The Continued Failure of the World Bank and IMF to Fully Assess the Impact of Their Advice on Poor People." Joint NGO Briefing Note.

Sechaba Consultants. 2004. "Lesotho: Poverty and Social Impact Analysis of Electricity Sector Reform." Report for World Bank, Sechaba Consultants, Maseru, Lesotho.

Wolfenson, J. D. 1997. "The Challenge of Inclusion." Annual Meeting Address, Hong Kong, September 23.

World Bank. Forthcoming. "The Development Policy Lending Retrospective." Operations, Policy and Country Services Report, World Bank, Washington, DC.

———. 2009a. "Assessing the Use of Poverty and Social Impact Analysis in World Bank Development Policy Loans." World Bank, Washington, DC.

———. 2009b. "Projects & Operations." http://go.worldbank.org/0FRO32VEI0.

———. 2008a. "Achieving Better Service Delivery through Decentralization in Ethiopia." World Bank Working Paper No. 131, World Bank, Washington, DC.

———. 2008b. "Good Practice Note: Using Poverty and Social Impact Analysis to Support Development Policy Operations." World Bank, Washington, DC.

———. 2008c. *The Impact of Macro-Economic Policies on Poverty and Income Distribution: Macro-Micro Evaluation Techniques and Tools.* Washington, DC: World Bank.

———. 2008d. "Mauritania: Poverty and Social Impact Analysis—Policy Note on Reforms to the Provision of Ancillary Services in the Mauritania Mining Sector." Report No. 40019-MR, World Bank, Washington, DC.

———. 2008e. "Poverty and Social Impact Analysis." http://www.worldbank.org/psia.

———. 2007a. "Bangladesh: Revival of Inland Water Transport: Options and Strategies." World Bank Policy Note. Report No. 38009, World Bank, Washington, DC.

———. 2007b. "Chairman's Summary: Fourth IDA-15 Meeting." Dublin, November 12–13. http://siteresources.worldbank.org/IDA/Resources/CSummaryDublin.pdf.

———. 2007c. "First Poverty Reduction Support Grant: Support to the Malawi Growth and Development Strategy." IDA Program Document, Report No. 40169-MW, World Bank, Washington, DC.

———. 2007d. "Northern Uganda Land Study: Analysis of Post-Conflict Land Policy and Land Administration—A Survey of IDP Return and Resettlement Issues and Lessons: Acholi and Lango Regions." Northern Uganda Recovery and Development Program Report, World Bank, Washington, DC.

———. 2007e. "Poverty and Environmental Impacts of Electricity Price Reforms in Montenegro." World Bank Policy Research Working Paper No. 4127, World Bank, Washington, DC.

———. 2007f. "Sierra Leone—Mining Sector Reform: A Strategic Environmental and Social Assessment." World Bank, Washington, DC.

———. 2007g. "Tools for Institutional, Political, and Social Analysis of Policy Reform: A Sourcebook for Development Practitioners." World Bank, Washington, DC.

———. 2007h. "Training and Advice on the Rwanda Poverty Analysis Macroeconomic Simulator (PAMS)." Report to World Bank and Republic of Rwanda Ministry of Finance and Economic Planning, Kigali, Rwanda.

———. 2007i. "Uruguay: Strengthening Participatory Monitoring and Evaluation of Social Policy: Report of Phase I." Report No. 40110-UY, World Bank, Washington, DC.

———. 2007j. "Yemen's Water Sector Reform Program: A Poverty and Social Impact Analysis." Report No. 43082, World Bank, Washington, DC.

———. 2006a. "Analyse des Impacts Sociaux et sur la Pauvreté des Reformes Envisagées dans les Domaines de l'Alimentation en Eau Potable et de l'Assainissement." [Morocco] World Bank, Washington, DC.

———. 2006b. *Analyzing the Distributional Impact of Reforms: Volume II: A Practitioner's Guide to Pension, Health, Labor Markets, Public Sector Downsizing, Taxation, Decentralization, and Macroeonomic Modeling.* Washington, DC: World Bank.

———. 2006c. "Cambodia: Halving Poverty by 2015? Poverty Assessment 2006." Report No. 35213-KH, World Bank, Washington, DC.

———. 2006d. "Côte d'Ivoire: Contributions à l'Analyse de la Pauvreté (Contributions to Poverty Analysis)." Report No. 36625-CI, World Bank, Washington, DC.

———. 2006e. "A Gender Analysis of Pension Reform Scenarios in Serbia." World Bank Report, Washington, DC.

———. 2006f. "Guyana: A Poverty and Social Impact Analysis of Changes in the Sugar Regime." World Bank Poverty and Social Impact Analysis, Washington, DC.

———. 2006g. "IBRD Program Document for a Proposed Loan in the Amount of €403 Million to the Republic of Turkey for a Programmatic Public Sector Development Policy Loan." Report No. 36274-TR, World Bank, Washington, DC.

———. 2006h. "Job Creation in Mozambique: Is Labor Law Reform the Answer?" PREM Report, World Bank, Washington, DC.

———. 2006i. "Local Government Taxation Reform in Tanzania: A Poverty and Social Impact Analysis: Report on Economic and Sector Work." Report No. 34900-TZ, World Bank, Washington, DC.

———. 2006j. "Making Government Work for the Poor." In *Making the New Indonesia Work for the Poor*, 221–66. Washington, DC: World Bank.

———. 2006k. "Making Social Protection Work for the Poor." In *Making the New Indonesia Work for the Poor*, 177–220. Washington, DC: World Bank.

———. 2006l. "Mauritania Poverty and Social Impact Assessment: Consumer Assessment of Reforms to the Provision of Ancillary Services in the Mauritania Mining Sector." PREM Report, World Bank, Washington, DC.

———. 2006m. "Nicaragua: The Impact of the Fiscal Equity Law Reform." In *Poverty and Social Impact Analysis of Reforms: Lessons and Examples of Implementations*, ed. Aline Coudouel, Anis A. Dani, and Stefano Paternostro, 29–66. Washington, DC: World Bank.

———. 2006n. *Poverty and Social Impact Analysis of Reforms: Lessons and Examples from Implementation*. Washington, DC: World Bank.

———. 2006o. "Poverty and Social Impact Analysis for the Water Sector Reform in Montenegro and Social Assessment for the Montenegro Tourism Development Project." Poverty and Social Impact Analysis, World Bank, Washington, DC.

———. 2006p. "Social Protection Options to Mitigate the Impact of Energy Sector Reforms in Tajikistan: A Poverty and Social Impact Analysis." Environmentally and Socially Sustainable Development Department Report, World Bank, Washington, DC.

———. 2006q. "Sri Lanka: Welfare Reform." In *Poverty and Social Impact Analysis of Reforms: Lessons and Examples of Implementations*, ed. Aline Coudouel, Anis A. Dani, and Stefano Paternostro, 149–212. Washington, DC: World Bank.

———. 2006r. "Tanzania: Crop Boards Reform." In *Poverty and Social Impact Analysis of Reforms: Lessons and Examples of Implementations,* ed. Aline Coudouel, Anis A. Dani, and Stefano Paternostro, 491–520. Washington, DC: World Bank.

———. 2006s. "Ukraine Energy and Poverty Note." Report to World Bank, Washington, DC.

———. 2005a. *Analyzing the Distributional Impact of Reforms: Volume I: A Practitioner's Guide to Monetary and Exchange Rate Policy, Utility Provision, Agricultural Markets, Land Policy, and Education*. Washington, DC: World Bank.

———. 2005b. "Democratic Republic of Congo: Economic and Sector Work: Governance and Service Delivery." Report No. 32205-ZR, World Bank, Washington, DC.

———. 2005c. "Egypt—Toward a More Effective Social Policy: Subsidies and Social Safety Net." Report No. 33550-EG. World Bank, Washington, DC.

———. 2005d. "El Salvador Poverty and Social Impact Analysis on CAFTA: A Partial Equilibrium Estimate of the Treaty's Welfare Impact on the Salvadoran Population." Working Paper No. 34069, World Bank, Washington, DC.

———. 2005e. "Improving Trade and Transport Efficiency—Understanding the Political Economy of Chittagong Port." Bangladesh Development Series Paper No. 6, World Bank, Washington, DC.

———. 2005f. "Indonesia—Poverty and Social Impact Analysis: Social Protection Reform." Summary document, World Bank, Washington, DC.

———. 2005g. "Indonesia: PSIA I—Fuel Subsidy." Summary document, World Bank, Washington, DC.

———. 2005h. "Mozambique: Poverty and Social Impact Analysis—Primary School Enrollment and Retention: The Impact of School Fees." Report No. 29423, World Bank, Washington, DC.

———. 2005i. "Nepal Poverty Assessment: Socio Economic Impact of Fuel Prices in Nepal." Background Paper, World Bank, Washington, DC.

———. 2005j. "Nicaragua—Desconcentración y Descentralización de los Servicios de Agua Potable y Alcantarillado—Análisis de Pobreza e Impacto Social." Final report, World Bank, Washington, DC.

———. 2005k. "Poverty and Social Impact Analysis of Sri Lanka's Land Policy Reforms: Socio-Economic Impact Assessment." Final report, World Bank, Washington, DC.

———. 2005l. "A Poverty and Social Impact Analysis of Three Reforms in Zambia: Land, Fertilizer, and Infrastructure." Social Development Papers, Paper No. 49, World Bank, Washington, DC.

————. 2005m. "République de Djibouti: Analyse d'Impact Social et Pauvreté Secteur Energétique." Report No. 32260-DJ, World Bank, Washington, DC.

————. 2005n. "Turkey Labor Market Study." Report No. 33254-TR, World Bank, Washington, DC.

————. 2004a. "Assessment of Potential Impacts of 'Social Land Concessions.' Final Report." Report No. 34475. World Bank, Washington, DC.

————. 2004b. "Benin—Cotton Sector Reforms: A Poverty and Social Impact Analysis." Report No. 29951-BJ, World Bank, Washington, DC.

————. 2004c. "Does Public Investment Help Spur Growth and Reduce Poverty in Nicaragua?" World Bank Poverty and Social Impact Analysis, Washington, DC.

————. 2004d. "Evaluation of the Distributional Impact of the Honduran Tax Reform." World Bank Report, Washington, DC.

————. 2004e. "Ghana Poverty and Social Impact Analysis: Electricity Tariffs: Phase I." World Bank, Washington, DC.

————. 2004f. "Good Practice Note: Poverty and Social Impact Analysis." World Bank, Washington, DC.

————. 2004g. "Identifying Opportunities to Increase Efficiency in the Trade and Transport Sectors." Draft Concept Note, World Bank, Washington, DC.

————. 2004h. "Malawi—Tobacco Sector Performance Audit: The Perceptions and Views of Smallholder Tobacco Farmers on the State of Play in the Tobacco Sector." Report to the World Bank, Washington, DC.

————. 2004i. "Nicaraguan Agriculture and CAFTA." World Bank Report, Washington, DC.

————. 2004j. "Operational Policy 8.60: Development Policy Lending." http://go.worldbank.org/YMN1C0RWR0.

————. 2004k. "Poverty and Social Impact Analysis of the Irrigation and Drainage Rehabilitation Projects and the Water Resource Management Project in Albania." World Bank Report, Washington, DC.

————. 2004l. "Rice Prices, Agricultural Input Subsidies, Transaction Costs, and Seasonality: A Multi-Market Model Poverty and Social Impact Analysis for Madagascar." Poverty and Social Impact Analysis, World Bank, Washington, DC.

————. 2004m. "Santé et Pauvreté en Mauritanie: Analyse et Cadre Stratégique de Lutte Contre la Pauvreté." Poverty and Social Impact Analysis, World Bank, Washington, DC.

————. 2004n. "Sharing Power: Lessons Learned from the Reform and Privatization of Moldova's Electricity Sector Poverty and Social Impact Analysis." Poverty and Social Impact Analysis, World Bank, Washington, DC.

————. 2004o. "World Bank Poverty and Social Impact Analysis: Impact of Hydrocarbon Price Increases—A Vision from the Perspective of MECOVI Surveys." Bolivia PSIA, World Bank, Washington, DC.

————. 2003a. "The Distributional Impact of the Nicaraguan Fiscal Equity Law." World Bank, Washington, DC.

————. 2003b. "District-Level Service Delivery in Rural Madagascar: Accountability in Health and Education." Working Paper, World Bank, Washington, DC.

————. 2003c. "From Goats to Coats: Institutional Reform in Mongolia's Cashmere Sector." Report No. 26240-MOG, World Bank, Washington, DC.

————. 2003d. "The Incidence of Public Education Spending in Nicaragua: The Impact of the Education for All–Fast Track Initiative." World Bank Report, Washington, DC.

————. 2003e. "Poverty and Social Impact Analysis: Indonesia Rice Tariff." World Bank Poverty and Social Impact Analysis, Washington, DC.

————. 2003f. "Reforming the Malawi Agricultural Development and Marketing Corporation: Synthesis Report of the Poverty and Social Impact Analysis." Report No. 27512, World Bank, Washington, DC.

————. 2003g. "Toolkit for Evaluating the Poverty and Distributional Impact of Economic Policies." http://go.worldbank.org/Q199F135V0.

————. 2003h. "A User's Guide to Poverty and Social Impact Analysis." http://go.worldbank.org/IR9SLBWTQ0.

———. 2002. "Examining the Social Impact of the Indonesian Financial Crisis Using a Micro-Macro Model." Paper presented at OECD seminar "How Are Globalisation and Poverty Interacting and What Can Governments Do about It?" Paris, December 10.

———. 2001a. "Adjustment Lending Retrospective." Working Paper No. 44666, World Bank, Washington, DC.

———. 2001b. "Concept Note: Social Impact Analysis (SIA) of Macroeconomic and Structural Policies." Draft document, World Bank, Washington, DC.

———. 2001c. "State Ownership and Labor Redundancy: Estimates Based on Enterprise-Level Data from Vietnam." World Bank Policy Research Working Paper No. 2599, World Bank, Washington, DC.

———. 2001d. "Utility Pricing and the Poor: Lessons from Armenia." World Bank Technical Paper No. 497, World Bank, Washington, DC.

———. 1987. "World Bank Manual Circular OP 87/88: Guidelines for Preparing and Processing Adjustment Loans and Credits." World Bank, Washington, DC.

World Bank, Government of Ethiopia, Irish Aid, UNICEF, USAID, WHO. 2007. *Reaching or Escaping the Challenge: Financing the Health MDGs in Ethiopia.* Washington, DC: World Bank.